Literary Genius

of the

OLD TESTAMENT

Oxford University Press

London   Edinburgh   Glasgow   Copenhagen
New York   Toronto   Melbourne   Cape Town
Bombay   Calcutta   Madras   Shanghai
Humphrey Milford Publisher to the UNIVERSITY

Literary Genius

OF THE

Old Testament

By

P. C. SANDS

HEAD MASTER OF POCKLINGTON SCHOOL, AND LATE FELLOW
OF ST. JOHN'S COLLEGE, CAMBRIDGE

'England became the people of a book, and
that book was the Bible.'

J. R. GREEN

OXFORD

At the Clarendon Press. A.D. 1926

Printed in England
At the OXFORD UNIVERSITY PRESS
By John Johnson
Printer to the University

PREFACE

THE main object of this book is explained in the introductory chapter. But it also aims at providing those who teach divinity to higher forms in schools with a subsidiary course of lessons to those usually taken for the School Certificate Examinations.

Years ago literary criticism and appreciation was little taught in schools, least of all in special relation to the Bible. Nor is it easy to teach, though books on the subject are now making their appearance. Boys, too, are not apt to be much interested in style. When they are told that a certain passage is a fine one, they are often content not to ask why. Yet literary appreciation is more and more insisted on in modern education, and even tested in examinations, and now that the study of the Old Testament has been revolutionized, it is important that as the teacher feels less inclined to give prominence to the mere facts of Jewish history, he should have the means of approaching the Old Testament from broader points of view, and one of these may well be the literary point of view. This book is a modest attempt to provide him with the means of giving interesting lessons on the literary genius of the Old Testament. The writer has already tried the lessons in class, and found they aroused interest, and that some excellent exercises were produced by pupils on the lines indicated at the end of various lessons. These exercises are not the least important part of the course, and the preparation for the lessons should also be done by the class.

19779

In studying the style, it is quite certain that other values, spiritual and historical, will simultaneously gain increased recognition, and whatever powers of criticism are awakened in the pupils, will certainly not be of the destructive kind. The story of Elijah and the poetry of Isaiah extort the fullest admiration only from those who appreciate style as well as matter.

The writer owes a very considerable debt to Peake's *Commentary on the Bible,* especially to the article in it upon ' The Bible as Literature ', by Professor Hudson. In fairness to himself, however, he would say that the outline and most of the details of this course of lessons were written before he saw the *Commentary,* and that he was fortunate to have selected for the lessons much the same subjects and mode of treatment as those touched upon in the excellent sketch referred to,—fortunate, because it was possible to embody the suggestions of an expert authority without re-casting or re-constructing. Other smaller debts are acknowledged in the footnotes.

P. C. S.

POCKLINGTON SCHOOL,
    May, 1924.

CONTENTS

I

INTRODUCTORY

In the following lessons an attempt will be made to analyse the main literary features of the Old Testament, to examine some of the most popular stories and poems, and the grounds upon which we admire them as literature.

This is well worth doing for several reasons, first because this aspect of the Old Testament was, until recently, very much ignored and neglected, whereas great utterances are usually as admirable for their form as for their matter, and the Old Testament is no exception to the rule. Those who hear the Old Testament read Sunday by Sunday will listen with increased enjoyment, when they associate with various passages ideas of literary beauty. Secondly, our greatest writers have owed a considerable debt to the style of the Old Testament through the Authorised Version, and the translation is one of the greatest works in the English tongue. Thirdly, the features of the Hebrew style may well be noted with a view to imitation by those who aspire to write effectively themselves. These features are not elusive. They are as strongly marked as the features of the Hebrew race itself, and to make oneself familiar with them is to learn some of the secrets of constructing a style.

Some account may well be expected of the race which produced the literature, and of how and when the various books came to be written. But there are now so many excellent handbooks and commentaries which give the results of recent research, that this preface may be of the briefest. A word is needed about the position of the Jews in the world's history. A short summary of the latest conclusions of scholars about the dates and authorship of the various books will perhaps be found useful. A word too upon the

literature as a whole, and upon the extraordinary
ion of so many writers upon one central idea, will
he limitations and the peculiar inspiration of the
genius.

(v) st a word about the Jews themselves. Books have
recently appeared upon the 'legacy of the Greeks' and the
'legacy of the Romans' to the human race. The legacy of
the Hebrews is even more important, if religious thought
counts for more than aesthetic ideals or political thought.
This legacy of the Hebrews is the literature represented to
us by the Bible. When we think of the Bible and the
prodigious effect it has had upon Europe, and then of the
nationality of the despised Jew, we are reminded of the difference between the power and influence of St. Paul on the one
hand, and of his physical insignificance in the eyes of his
congregation at Corinth on the other. 'His letters', they
said, 'are weighty and strong, but his bodily presence is
weak, and his speech of no account'. The literature of the
Jew is weighty and strong, but the presence of the race in
the flesh was weak, and in the councils of the nations their
speech was of little account. So far as we know, some
Hebrew tribes migrated in what is known as the Exodus
from Egypt about 1250 B.C., after a period of oppression by
Rameses II. These tribes, after entering Canaan, lived in
the manner reflected in the Book of Judges, in considerable
disunion, and with very primitive beliefs in family gods and
images, but with the beginnings of a national consciousness,
which had been created by Moses, and was linked with a
belief in a tribal God, Jehovah. About two hundred years
later the tribes had been welded together by Saul, so that
David and Solomon reigned over a single nation. The split
into two kingdoms about 900 B.C. was a blow to further
expansion. In the next three centuries Israel and Judah
were in the unhappy position of small buffer states between
Assyria and Egypt, and first the Northern kingdom, then in
586 B.C. the kingdom of Judah was ended by the capture
of its capital and the transportation of its inhabitants.

Even when some of the exiles were allowed to return, and rebuild the temple and the city walls of Jerusalem, the restored community, strengthened in its devotion to Jehovah, enjoyed but a short rest, in which however it did the great work of collecting, editing, and adding to the sacred books, in which their religious traditions were henceforth preserved. In 168 B.C. Antiochus Epiphanes tried to suppress their worship, and after great persecutions and sufferings the unhappy people was barely rescued by the heroism of the Maccabees. In 63 B.C. began their dependence upon Rome, who governed them with as much difficulty as the British governed the Irish.

The Jews had by now come to contrast their purer worship of the one God with the idolatries and baser worships of all other peoples, and to separate themselves spiritually from the Gentiles, as the Greeks had previously distinguished themselves intellectually from the ' barbarians '. They alone had a part in the true Jehovah, to them alone belonged the true wisdom, compared with which the culture and philosophy of other peoples were of no account. They alone lived in righteousness. Other religions entailed sin and degradation.

The Jew, therefore, was as proud of his religion as the Roman of his empire, and each heartily despised the other. Rome was tolerant, but could not understand the religious attitude of the Jew. The Jew was intolerant of any encroach-ment of heathen rites or symbols, like the Roman eagles, in the neighbourhood of their sacred city. Continuous friction ended in the destruction of Jerusalem in 71 A.D., when the Romans 'took away the Jews' place and nation '. So ended the history of ' this repulsive people ', as Tacitus called them, for whom, as for the Greeks, the later Roman poets had only words of contempt, Horace for the circumcised Jew, Juvenal for the ' hungry little Greek '. Yet both these despised mem-bers of the Roman Empire left their mark upon it as no other peoples did. The Greek, it was already admitted, had 'taken captive his fierce conqueror ', and within the next three centuries the monotheism of the Jews, the belief in one

God, which the prophets had steadily evolved, and to which final literary expression was given during and after the Captivity, was through Christian propaganda to dominate the Roman Empire. The proud Roman, who had learnt to think aesthetically in Greek, was before long to think spiritually in Hebrew.

The Jewish Jehovah, 'who cared and loved, who rejoiced and grieved, who rewarded and punished and forgave, a very human God, but yet strictly One, the sole deity of all the world, a personal God, but also a God of spirit, not of flesh and blood, a God of whom no image or picture might be adored or even made, . . . a holy God, but withal approachable, an awful God, and yet the Father of his people,'[1] banished all the images from the temples of Italy and was acknowledged by Roman and Goth in succession.

To have thought out this idea of Godhead was the great, the miraculous achievement of the Hebrews. This strict monotheism they had, since the Exile, 'stereotyped for preservation and placed upon a legal basis', so that at a time 'when all nationalities and all bonds of religion were beginning to be broken up in the seeming chaos of the Graeco-Roman Empire, the Jews stood out like a rock in the midst of the ocean.'[2]

(*b*) Next we must briefly summarize the development of the literature, through which this monotheism was expressed.

The Bible is not the whole of the literature of the Hebrews. Lost books are referred to, such as the book of Jasher, and poetry of a more secular type existed, even perhaps before Moses, such as the Song of Lamech, the curse on Canaan, and the blessing of Shem and Japhet. Those who collected the books of the Old Testament and edited them were interested only in the religious traditions of the race, and omitted what a secular historian might have been glad to include.

The literature of a people usually begins with poetry, prose is developed later.

[1] Montefiore. [2] Wellhausen.

Production of the Books.

	Position in modern Bible.	Approximate date.

Examples of fragments of early POETRY are the Song of the Well, the Song of Lamech, and the others just mentioned above. More complete odes are the Song of Deborah, and the Lament for Saul and Jonathan, written by David himself (cf. the fragment of his elegy on Abner, 2 Sam. iii. 33).

Num. xxi. 17 f. Gen. iv. 23 f. — Perhaps before Moses.

Judg. v. — Time of Judges.

2 Sam. i. 19 ff. — Time of David from 1010 B.C.

The Blessing of Jacob may also belong to the time of David, and some scholars put Miriam's Ode about the same time, though others date it in its final form after the Exile.

Gen. xlix. — ,,

Exodus xv. — ?

David may have composed other odes besides those quoted, but the Psalms are of late composition and not to be ascribed to him, as the titles at their head suggest.

HISTORY and BIOGRAPHY probably started in Solomon's reign. Up to then the nation was busy struggling for its existence. Stories of David's court were perhaps the first to be reduced to writing, and of the time immediately previous, viz. of Samuel and Saul, and David before he was king. Then records of the conquest of Canaan were collected, and of the time of the Judges.

2 Sam. ix–xx, 1 Kings i f. — Solomon's reign and after, from 970 B.C.

Rest of 1 and 2 Sam.

The next important documents were those now known as J and E, sources of the present Pentateuch, one by a Judaean writer, the other

Parts of the Pentateuch. — Probably before 750 B.C.

Production of the Books.	*Position in modern Bible.*	*Approximate date.*

by a writer of the Northern kingdom.

ANNALS also began to be compiled under the monarchy, and combined with stories to form history. The stories of Elijah and Elisha relieve the official records of the Books of Kings. — 1 and 2 Kings. — About the 8th century B.C.

PROPHECY. The prophets began to deliver their addresses when the Assyrians started to threaten Israel, and they afterwards reduced them to writing. Prophecy was temporarily silenced upon the death of Isaiah. — Amos, and Hosea. — 760–735 B.C.; 1 Isaiah (most of ch. i–xxxv) and Micah. — 740–690 B.C.

LAW. In the reign of Josiah a roll or book of Law was found, which is now identified with part of Deuteronomy (roughly ch. xii–xxvi). It was probably produced in Hezekiah's reign, but did not reach its present dimensions till the end of the Exile. — Deut. xii–xxvi. — Discovered in Josiah's reign 622 B.C.

Prophecy is resumed with Zephaniah, with Nahum, who denounces the doomed Nineveh, and with Jeremiah. — Zephaniah, Nahum, Jeremiah. — Fl. 630 B.C.; Fl. 610 B.C.; Fl. 605 B.C.

Fall of Jerusalem 586 B.C.

From this point the literature of the Old Testament, which has hitherto been, so to speak, in embryo, began to take its final form through collecting and editing and the addition of many notable books.

Production of the Books.

It was during the Exile that Judges, Samuel, and Kings were edited from the standpoint of the ideas preserved in Deuteronomy. Prophecy was continued by Ezekiel, who taught theology systematically to the exiles, and by 2 Isaiah, who comforted them with the prospect of return.

Poetry is represented during this period by part of the Lamentations, and by many of the Psalms, prose by that source of the Pentateuch now known as P, while Job, which is dated by many about this time, is an example of a kind of literature usually grouped together nowadays as 'Wisdom'.

There was also much compiling of laws, and recording of ritual.

After the Exile the prophets Haggai and Zechariah encouraged the restored community in Judaea, followed by Malachi, 3 Isaiah, and Obadiah.

The growth of Judaism, hard and stern, forbidding foreign marriages, and impatient for the destruction of the Gentile world, prompted the writing of Ruth and Jonah in protest, 'perfect examples of the short story', pointing respectively to the example of Ruth the Moabitess and Boaz, and to the imaginary experience of Jonah and the wicked Nineveh.

Position in modern Bible.	Approximate date.
Ezekiel.	592–570 B.C.
Isaiah xl–lv.	About 540 B.C.
Lamentations, Psalms.	About 580 B.C. and after.
The rest of the Pentateuch.	(Uncertain.)
Job.	(Uncertain.)
Haggai and Zechariah, i–viii.	520 B.C.
Malachi and Is. lvi–lxvi, Obadiah.	About 450 B.C.
Ruth and Jonah.	5th century.

Production of the Books.	*Position in modern Bible.*	*Approximate date.*
Last among the prophets come Joel and the second part of Zechariah, while the history, left unfinished in Kings, is rounded off by Chronicles, Ezra, and Nehemiah, originally forming one continuous book by the same writer, some scribe, who lived at the beginning of the fourth century, B.C.	Joel, and Zechariah, ix–xiv.	4th century.
	Chronicles, Ezra, and Nehemiah.	300 B.C.
The Song of Songs is usually dated in the third century B.C., and Ecclesiastes about 200 B.C. Proverbs was also compiled after the Exile, though earlier collections were embodied in the book.	Song of Songs.	3rd century.
	Ecclesiastes, Proverbs.	200 B.C. Uncertain.
Daniel and Esther date from the period of the Maccabees. The object of the author of Daniel was to encourage the Jewish patriots against the king of Syria, (*a*) by representing the events of his own time as predicted by Daniel after a vision (see especially ch. ix), (*b*) by relating heroism in defence of the national worship during the Exile.	Daniel.	About 165 B.C.
The book of Esther presents a story of the Exile as a motive for the Feast of Purim.	Esther.	Last century B.C.

(Habakkuk has not been included above owing to the different dates ascribed to its various parts.)

(*c*) Lastly, a few words must be added about the tone of the Old Testament and the concentration of so many writers upon one main theme, which gives its unity to the Bible.

Our own Puritans, the Roundheads of Cromwell, and the Scottish Covenanters, who saturated themselves with the spirit and language of the Old Testament, will remind us of that religious fervour which characterizes the zealot, which makes serious his every thought, which colours his speech, rules his least action from morning to night, and gives him a set cast of countenance. Bigotry, vindictiveness, and even ruthlessness, may go with it, indeed to the warm-blooded Semitic Jew they belonged as the heritage of his race, and these prompted such outbursts as the curses of Psalms lxix, cix, and cxxxvii (v. 9), which the Church is now preparing to expurgate from its Psalter. But this intense spiritual consciousness in spite of the accompanying faults and flaws commands the deepest respect. In fact it constitutes a special kind of genius. The Old Testament is the outcome of the concentrated thought of a number of writers who 'brooded upon God', 'As the hart panteth after the water-brooks, so panteth my soul after thee, O God', 'I remember thee upon my bed', says the Psalmist. Jehovah's identity is tirelessly emphasized, 'I am the Lord', 'I the Lord thy God have spoken it', 'The Lord, he is God, there is none else'. The new ideals of purity of worship and holiness which inspired these writers, and their reformed views upon ritual, colour their accounts of the kings of old. 'Hezekiah did that which was right . . . he removed the high places.' In writing of the great men of old, they present them as saints rather than as heroes—it is their attitude to Jehovah and Jehovah's attitude to them that are of primal importance, their spiritual experience, not their temporal greatness, though that may be an additional source of satisfaction to the writer to dwell upon. Thus Enoch 'walked with God', Abraham was the 'friend of God', Moses 'talked with God face to face', Samuel 'grew on and was in favour with God and man', David 'was a man after God's own heart', Solomon's vision and prayer precede the account of his magnificence. Daniel prays to God three times a day. Job was 'perfect and upright, and feared the Lord God'. So,

/hile the ideal man of the Greeks with their love of beauty was the καλὸς κἀγαθός, the 'beautiful and good' man, and the Roman ideal was the *vir gravis*, or dependable man, equally suitable for a governing race, the Jewish ideal was the righteous man, the righteous servant of Jehovah. The greatest utterance put into the mouth of their greatest man, Moses, is characteristically humble and befitting the saint. When asked by Joshua to forbid two men prophesying in the camp, he replied, 'Art thou jealous for my sake? Would God that all the Lord's people were prophets, and that the Lord would put his spirit upon them.'[1]

Such men are made to speak of the nation's enemies as God's enemies, 'Rise up, Lord, and let thine enemies be scattered',[2] is the prayer put into the mouth of Moses, when the people resumed their march through the desert every morning. God is behind every action of man. If Samson slew his thousands, the 'spirit of God came upon him'. The sleep of Saul in his tent is 'a deep sleep from the Lord'. In the horrors of civil war, it is the Lord who smote Benjamin before the other tribes. The slaughter of a tribe or the looting of a city is ordered by the Lord, we read, because God absorbs the work of everybody in the Old Testament. 'There are no odes to Moses or Joshua or David; these and all the great prophets and leaders are forgotten in the absorbing brilliance of Jehovah's glory.'[3] In fact the whole nation is conceived to have been set apart by destiny as a nation of priests, serving Jehovah, and the past history of the people was edited in this belief.

It is interesting to note how the deep religious tone colours the everyday intercourse of the people, as it is described in the Old Testament, their daily greetings, 'God be gracious unto thee, my son', or as Boaz says to the reapers, 'The Lord be with you', and they reply, 'The Lord bless thee'; their good wishes for a successful errand, 'God Almighty give you grace before the man'; their oaths, 'As the Lord

---

[1] Num. xi. 28. [2] Num. x. 35.
[3] *Life and Literature of the Ancient Hebrews*, L. Abbott.

liveth ', ' God forbid ', those wonderful blessings, 'The Lord bless thee and keep thee, the Lord make his face to shine upon thee, and be gracious unto thee, the Lord lift up his countenance upon thee and give thee peace '.[1]

Such, then, is the tone of the Old Testament and its dominant idea. The scope, therefore, of the literature of the Old Testament is narrower than that of other national literatures preserved for us. The belief that all things began and ended in Jehovah restricted philosophical speculation and checked intellectual curiosity, such as stimulated the Greeks. Philosophy is thus represented only by the books of 'Wisdom', so-called, which do not inquire deeply into causes, nor put together connected reasonings. Another kind of literature that we miss is Comedy, which was incompatible with the serious temperament of the race. (See the chapter on Irony.) Tragic Drama is also wanting. Dramatic power is shown in Job, but there is no drama as we know it. Poetry is represented by lyrics, and oratory by the speeches of Moses. History and biography bulk largely, but the history is mainly stories of great men. The features which will be treated in these lessons as the most striking in the literature of the Old Testament are :

(*a*) *in Prose,*

    i. The vividness and dramatic qualities of the stories just mentioned.

    ii. The sublime descriptions of God, revealing himself to his chosen servants.

(*b*) *in Poetry,*

    The wonderful imagery and literary figures of the lyrics, and their manner of expressing emotional and devotional experience, both personal and national.

But unique in literature is the series of Hebrew *prophecies,* many of which by their rhythm and balance of thought

---

[1] Num. vi. 24 .

resemble poetry rather than prose, and show the same wealth of imagery, a great power of pleading and invective, and a lofty conception of God. The most notable things in these prophecies may well be treated along with the poetry, as also those of the book of Job. Lastly examples will be given of the *gnomic style* of the Books of Wisdom, a term which is sometimes allowed to include the book of Job, but otherwise is applied to a store of wise sayings, now grouped round a central thought, now a mere miscellany of proverbs.

Lesson I [1]

The ART of STORY-TELLING

THE narratives of the Old Testament, especially of the Pentateuch, have now been very carefully analysed by scholars, and the result has been to distinguish between the following sources :

(a) Two ancient sources using different names for God, namely, Elohim, translated by 'God', and Yahveh, translated by 'Lord', two sources similar in style, and called by scholars for convenience E and J respectively.

(b) A later authority who writes in a more formal style and makes great use of the phrase, 'These are the generations of . . . ', called by scholars P.

(c) The original document of Deuteronomy, which scholars have labelled D.

For the peculiarities of these different authors the reader is recommended to various commentaries on the Pentateuch. It is only the broader differences of style that concern us here, and especially those of J and E. P deals largely with the priestly code, and his style is dull, though sometimes realistic enough, as when he describes Abraham's long-drawn-out barter for the burying-place of Sarah, which reminds us of the bartering in an Oriental bazaar (Gen. xxiii). P has his long genealogies, lists of names, and constantly recurring formulae. His account of the creation, punctuated by the phrase 'God saw that it was good' (Gen. i), may be contrasted with the one which follows (ii. 4, second part of the verse, to

---

[1] The Bible should be at hand for reference throughout.

v. 24). P, less primitive than J, regards God as a Spirit. J, on the other hand, 'is most vivid and bold, speaking of God without reserve in terms applicable to men; He walks, smells, comes down from heaven, wrestles, &c.' E again 'is more reserved. God speaks to man not face to face, but through dreams and angelic visitors.' [1]

The editor who pieced together these different accounts, while sometimes leaving long passages from one of them, more often joins them in such a way that a story like that of Joseph cannot be dissected without spoiling the charm of the tale, and yet leaves small inconsistencies and repetitions that the reader could wish removed.

It is to J and in a less degree to E that we owe the best stories of the Pentateuch, if not of the Old Testament. Dr. Driver[2] speaks of the lightness of J's touch. 'With a few strokes he paints a scene, which, before he has finished, is impressed indelibly upon the reader's memory. In ease and grace his narratives are unsurpassed; everything is told with precisely the amount of detail required, the narrative never lingers and the reader's interest is sustained to the close.'

The chief qualities of these stories of the Pentateuch, as of the narrative of David's life, in Samuel, and the stories of Ruth, Elijah, and Elisha, &c., are the qualities of all good early narrative, and those who know Homer will be reminded of the vividness of many a Homeric scene. They are:

   i. *Perfection of simplicity and vivid picturesqueness.*

   ii. *Homely realism and concreteness.*

   iii. *Absence of elaboration and of descriptive details of character, scenery, dress, &c.*

   iv. *Dramatic power, due to their rapidity, use of dialogue, climaxes.*

---

[1] Lanchester, *The Old Testament*, p. 14.

[2] *Literature of the Old Testament.* Chaytor, *Story of Israel and Judah*, gives an example, 'The heaven was black with clouds and wind, and there was a great rain', and remarks, 'This is a more impressive description of a gathering and bursting storm than pages of detail would furnish'.

Abraham and the Strangers.

As an example of the first two qualities, the picturesque simplicity and the homely realism of these earlier narratives, let us take Abraham's reception of the three strangers, in Genesis xviii.

This passage has been aptly compared with Achilles' reception of the envoys of Agamemnon, in Homer, *Iliad* ix.[1] It will be worth while to put them side by side:

Gen. xviii. 1-9.	Homer, *Il.* ix. 185-220.
And the Lord appeared unto him by the oaks of Mamre, as he sat in the tent door in the heat of the day;	(Ajax and Odysseus go as envoys to appease the wrath of Achilles.)
and he lift up his eyes and looked, and, lo, three men stood over against him : and when he saw them, he ran to meet them from the tent door, and bowed himself to the earth,	And they came to the huts and ships of the Myrmidons, and found their king taking his pleasure of a loud lyre, fair, of curious work, with a silver cross-bar upon it; . . . therein he was delighting his soul, and singing the glories of heroes. And over against him sate Patroclus alone in silence, watching till Aeacides should cease from singing.
and said, My lord, if now I have found favour in thy sight, pass not away, I pray thee, from thy servant:	
let now a little water be fetched, and wash your feet, and rest yourselves under the tree :	So the twain came forward, and noble Odysseus led the way, and they stood before his face ; and Achilles sprang up with the lyre in his hand, and left the seat where he was sitting, and in like manner Patroclus, when he beheld the men, arose. Then Achilles fleet of foot greeted them and said, 'Welcome, verily ye are friends that are come . . .
and I will fetch a morsel of bread, and comfort ye your heart; after that ye shall pass on : forasmuch as ye are come to your servant. And they said, So do as thou hast said.	
And Abraham hastened into the tent unto Sarah, and said, Make ready quickly three measures of fine meal, knead it, and make cakes.	So spake noble Achilles and led them forward, and made them sit on settles and carpets of purple ; and anon he spake to Patroclus,
And Abraham ran unto the herd, and fetched a calf tender and good, and gave it unto the servant ; and he hasted to dress it.	'Bring forth a greater bowl, thou son of Menoitius ; mingle stronger drink, and prepare each man a cup, for dearest of
And he took butter and milk, and the calf which he had	

[1] See Peake's *Commentary on the Bible* (T. C. and E. C. Jack), p. 21.

Gen. xviii. 1–9 (*continued*).

dressed, and set it before them ; and he stood by them under the tree, and they did eat.

And they said unto him, Where is Sarah thy wife? And he said, Behold, in the tent.

Homer, *Il.* ix. 185–220 (*continued*).

men are these that are under my roof.'

So said he, and Patroclus hearkened to his dear comrade. He cast down a great fleshing-block in the firelight, and laid thereon a sheep's back and a fat goat's, and a great hog's chine rich in fat. And Automedon held them for him, while Achilles carved. Then he sliced well the meat and pierced it through with spits, and Menoitius's son, that godlike hero, made the fire burn high. Then when the fire was burned down and the flame waned, he scattered the embers and laid the spits thereover, resting them on the spitracks, when he had sprinkled them with holy salt.

Then, when he had roasted the meat and apportioned it to the platters, Patroclus took bread and dealt it forth on the table in fair baskets, and Achilles dealt the meat. And he sat him over against godlike Odysseus by the other wall . . .[1]

Note one or two common features of these two scenes of hospitality :

(*a*) The simplicity of style agrees with the simplicity of life and thought. At this early stage the simplest things which a man did were of general interest ; life was fresh and new. The chiefs, Abraham or Achilles, and their closest companions, Sarah the wife or Patroclus the bosom friend, prepare the meal themselves, and the simple and homely details of the preparation of the meal are the primitive counterpart of the elaborate descriptions of rich banquets that later writers introduce for their more 'civilized' readers.

[1] Butcher and Lang's translation.

(*b*) The details are like the few but suggestive lines of a simple drawing; they are picturesque, they immediately go to form a picture for us.

Genesis.	Homer.
' He sat in the tent door in the heat of the day.'	'Over against him sate Patroclus alone in silence, watching . . .
'He ran to meet them and bowed himself.'	' Achilles sprang up amazed *with the lyre in his hand.*'
'Let a little water be fetched and wash your feet.'	'Bring forth a greater bowl, thou son of Menoitius, and prepare each man a cup.'
Thus the scene and Oriental welcome.	So the corresponding Greek welcome.

The preparation of the meal is followed with a keen and healthy interest as of schoolboys :

' A calf tender and good.'	' A great hog's chine, rich in fat.'
'Three measures of *fine* meal.'	'Automedon held them for him, while Achilles carved. . . .'

The host takes his position at the table :

' He stood by them under the tree.'	' And he sate him over against godlike Odysseus by the other wall.'
(The Oriental waits upon the strangers in this case.)	

(*c*) The details by their fidelity to life, their 'homely realism and concreteness', give the impression that the writer himself lived before the kind of life that he describes had entirely disappeared. It sometimes happens that a later writer, used to the civilization of towns, tries to reproduce some incident from this more primitive kind of life without recapturing its freshness and realism. The difference in the story-telling is then very marked. A well-known instance may be quoted from classical sources. In Homer (*Od.* x. 148–72), Odysseus returning from scouting on a hill sees a stag, which ' some god taking pity on him in his loneliness, sent across his very path '. A very realistic account follows of the way in which Odysseus slew this stag. This incident is handled by the Roman poet

Vergil, the court poet of Augustus, in his *Aeneid*[1]; Vergil's hero Aeneas kills seven stags with bow and arrow, a very improbable feat, and while in Homer's story you can follow the whole process, from the cast of the spear to the depositing of the beast on the shore, Vergil leaves so many things unexplained that you feel that he was not interested in this performance of his hero (see below).[2]

The historical books of the Old Testament continue this picturesqueness and graphic power. Sections of the history of the kings in Samuel are attributed to the same source as the stories of the Pentateuch, and show the same style and method. Stories have always been popular in the East, and the history consists largely of stories of the greatest men. The books of Chronicles, it is true, contain genealogies and official lists and annals, but the bulk of the history is told in story form, like the account of the patriarchs, with the same picturesqueness and realism. The call of the child Samuel, the election of Saul, the modest giant, who 'hid himself amongst the stuff', the combat of David and Goliath, the last farewell scene between David and Jonathan, and the parable of Nathan to David will occur to the mind at once as instances among many. All are marked by vivid and faithful detail and the same clear and simple style. Stories from the books of Kings will be quoted to illustrate other qualities of story-telling. When we come to Chronicles, however, a later compilation altogether, with its genealogies, official lists, and annals, the style is no longer the same.

The Story of the Stag-Slaying in Homer and Vergil.

In Homer it is as follows: 'He was coming down from his pasture in the woodland to the river to drink, for *the might of the sun was sore upon him*. And as he came up from out of the stream, I smote him *in the spine in the middle of the*

[1] I, 188 ff.

[2] This should be examined at greater length at the end of the lesson. *Preparation* (for lesson 2). Read Ruth, especially chapter ii, and 2 Kings iv.

back, and the brazen shaft went clean through him, and *with a moan* he fell in the dust.   Then *I set my foot upon him, and drew forth the brazen shaft, and laid it on the ground and let it lie.*'

Note the completeness of the details of the action.   Two reasons are given to explain the good luck of Odysseus in getting so near to the stag, the pity of the god, and the stag's thirst induced by the heat.   To stalk a stag is not easy, and Odysseus points out that he happened upon it just as it was leaving the stream.

As the stag was a big one, and Odysseus had to carry it to the ship, he ' broke withies and willow twigs, and wove a rope *a fathom in length,* well twisted from end to end, and bound together the feet of the huge beast, and went to the black ship, *bearing him across my neck, and leaning on a spear,* for it was in no wise possible to carry him on my shoulder with one hand, for he was a mighty quarry'.   Even a hero of many great feats has his limitations in this realistic kind of narrative.   'And I threw him down before the ship.'   One can almost hear the sigh of relief, as he dropped him.

All this action one can watch from end to end; the methods of Robinson Crusoe will occur to us.

Now take the same incident reproduced by a poet who was less interested in these primitive scenes, but felt his hero must be homeric.   Aeneas must have his stag-slaying too. He has clambered up a rocky hill, just as Odysseus did, leaving his crews on the beach.   From this rock he sees three stags at a distance straying on the shore, followed by the whole herd :

'At once he took his stand, and caught up a bow and fleet arrows, which true Achates chanced to be carrying.' (His squire, Achates, was last mentioned as busy starting a fire, and his attendance upon Aeneas seems to be an afterthought.)   'And he lays low, first the leaders of the herd, then the meaner sort, and scatters with his pursuing shafts the whole rout among the leafy woods ; nor stays his hand till he stretches on earth seven huge bodies, and *makes the sum of them even with the ships.* Then he returns to the haven and gives all his comrades their shares. The wine he next portions out . . . '

This is a very different kind of story-telling. The details in which the poet improves upon the original story all make his tale more improbable, for instance, to shoot *seven* stags at a distance with arrows (because there happened to be seven crews wanting a meal), is a feat that few deerstalkers would credit. The stags would soon be out of range. The details that he omits are just those that make for realism—the chance encounter of Odysseus and the stag, as he was drawing near the ship, and as the stag was leaving the stream, the moan of the stag as it fell, the drawing out of the spear, and especially the trussing and carrying home of the animal. It is not explained how Aeneas and Achates carried the 'seven huge bodies' from a distance to the camp. Presumably the crews would have to go for them. Vergil was not interested sufficiently to explain.

Lesson 2

The ART of STORY-TELLING (continued)

Absence of Elaboration and Descriptive Details, e.g. of Character, Scenery, and Dress.

The third feature of these stories is the absence of all details *not essential to the action of the story.* The 'fundamentals' only are given. There is no analysis of character or description of scenery for its own sake. Joseph's home and his person are not described at all, as they would have been in a modern novel, and his 'coat of many colours', or, as it is more correctly rendered, 'long-sleeved' coat, is mentioned because of its connexion with Jacob's favouritism, and its influence upon the plot.[1]

[1] It was a coat unsuited for work, and suggests that Joseph was kept idle, while his brothers worked.

Ruth.

Take as the next example the story of Ruth, the little picture of Jewish life in the time of the Judges.

(1) A single verse supplies the setting of the story:

'It came to pass, in the days when the judges judged, that there was a famine in the land . . .' (or 'once upon a time' . . . as we say).

This simple beginning has been contrasted with that of the book of Esther, which represents a later stage in the evolution of the art of story-writing. There the elaborate description of the feast will be noted, designed to bring out the magnificence of the court.[1]

(2) The story is presented without comment or moralizing:

The only exception is where the writer stops to explain an obscure custom (iv. 7). Little is said about character or motive. What the actors say and do is set down, and the reader draws his own conclusions about them.

For example, Ruth's beauty that attracted Boaz is left to be imagined. 'A mighty man of wealth' is sufficient to introduce the hero. His courtesy and kindness is implied in the action.

(3) Though the story is a love-story, the romance of Boaz and Ruth, it contains no direct mention of love whatever. The symptoms indeed may be noted. For instance, after Boaz has noticed Ruth, and made careful inquiries about her, he bids her keep in his field, 'Go not elsewhere', 'glean . . . and use the water provided'; later on, he invites her to share the lunch provided, and actually waits upon her himself, 'reached her parched corn', as she sat among the reapers,[2] great condescension on the part of the lord of the manor to a foreign-born helper; he cannot rest, he next tells his young men to let her glean among the sheaves as well as what the reapers had left. Another thought strikes him; 'Let fall handfuls on purpose', is his next order. When Ruth claims his

[1] Prof. Hudson, in Peake's *Commentary*, p. 22.   [2] ii. 14, A. V.

protection and hand according to the Jewish law (iii. 10), he thanks her for her condescension and kindness in preferring himself to the younger men, and when Naomi, who had questioned Ruth closely (ii. 19 ff.), hears of a further present from Boaz, she says with confidence, 'The man will not rest until he have finished the thing this day'; she had heard enough to satisfy her, and knew that Boaz would make sure of his bride (iii. 18).

The simplicity of the diction,[1] which is a special feature of these stories, should be noted by the way, as the story of Ruth provides one of the greatest examples. Direct speech is more simple and natural than reported speech, and the genius of the English translators has given us a style in the authorized version, which is the despair of all imitators. Read over several times Ruth's words to Naomi in vv. 16, 17, short, simple, concrete words of the commonest kind, until the exquisite balance and rhythm have made themselves felt. Notice for instance how the rhythm is varied by the change of order in v. 17:

v. 16, whither thou goest, I will go, and where thou lodgest, I will lodge . . .

v. 17, where thou diest, *will I* die, and there *will I* be buried . . .

Notice also the final monosyllables of almost equal weight that end the speech:

'if aught but death part thee and me.

Even the binding oath is the simplest and most restrained form of oath:

'The Lord do so to me and more also, if . . .'

Such is the story of Ruth, a simple picture of fidelity and love without any elaboration or analysis of character or description of the actors. Other emotions and virtues are treated with the same restraint in all these early narratives. Brave deeds born of gratitude or loyalty are told as though the narrator were unconscious of the heroism, as in the classic epitaph on the Greek heroes of Thermopylae, the

See Chapter X.

band of the three hundred, who held up the Persian host for
days, and died in the forlorn hope :

> 'Stranger, tell the Lacedaemonians, that we lie here obedient
> to their laws.'

They had done merely what they had been told to do, there
was no particular merit in that, the 'unprofitable servants'
of the New Testament.[1]

Saul and Jabesh-gilead.

For instance, King Saul, newly elected, rescued the people
of Jabesh-gilead from a terrible fate (1 Sam. xi). No mention
is made of their gratitude until, at the end of his reign, when
he fell in battle and his body was hung up on the walls of
Beth-shan by the Philistines, we find three very simple verses
added by the chronicler, at the very end of the book :

> 'And when the inhabitants of Jabesh-gilead heard concerning
> him that which the Philistines had done to Saul, all the valiant
> men arose, and went all night, and took the body of Saul and the
> bodies of his sons from the wall of Beth-shan, and they came to
> Jabesh, and burnt them there. And they took their bones and
> buried them under the tamarisk tree in Jabesh, and fasted seven
> days.' (1 Sam. xxxi. 11–13.)

Much is left out here, the grief and indignation of the men of
Jabesh, all comment on their bravery, and the difficulties
of their exploit in the territory of the conquerors, and no
reference is made to their previous deliverance by Saul as a
motive.[2]

Rizpah.

In 2 Sam. xxi. 8–11, we find a woman named Rizpah
losing her two sons to satisfy a vendetta against the house
of Saul. They were 'hung up unto the Lord' by the
Gibeonites with David's consent, at the beginning of barley
harvest.

> 'And Rizpah the daughter of Aiah took sackcloth, and spread
> it for her upon the rock, from the beginning of harvest until

[1] St. Luke xvii. 10.

[2] Hereward the Wake's similar end and the recovery of his head from
the Normans will occur to those who have read Kingsley's novel.

water was poured upon them from heaven; and she suffered neither the birds of the air to rest on them by day, nor the beasts of the field by night.'

A lonely mountain at night time, beasts and birds of prey all round, and a woman watching the bodies of her sons with burning eyes—the mother's devotion needed no comment, but it was reported to David, we are told. ' It was told David what Rizpah had done.'

The Lady of Shunem.

Yet this simple restrained style, without description or comment, vividly presents the broader traits of character. No character could be more clearly outlined than that of the lady of Shunem who was hospitable to Elisha (2 Kings iv). She is married to an old husband and naturally takes the initiative (vv. 9, 22–23, cf. also v. 13), and she is a woman of strong convictions with the reticence that often goes with them. She knows her own mind and keeps her own counsel, a practical woman. She will name no reward for her hospitality; preferment at court does not appeal to her (vv. 13, 14). When her child dies of sunstroke, she shuts up her grief, and cannot discuss it with her husband (' It shall be well ', v. 23), or with Gehazi (' It is well ', v. 26). Her sorrow is speechless before Elisha himself (v. 27), till she at last gives vent to a couple of sentences of reproach for the motherhood given and so soon bereaved. She will not follow Gehazi. He has not the 'root of the matter', and if Elisha chooses such a servant, her instinct tells her that God will not. So she prevails on Elisha to come himself. When her child is restored ' she went in and fell at his feet, and bowed herself to the ground, and took up her son and went out '. It is a fine touch that her gratitude, like her grief, should be expressed silently.

Exercise. Tell the story of Queen Eleanor and the release of Edward III's prisoners at Calais, in the style and diction of early Hebrew narrative.

Preparation (for next lesson). Read 2 Kings ix, 2 Sam. xvii, xviii, and, if time allows, Gen. xl–xlii.

III

Lesson 3 [1]

DRAMATIC POWER

DRAMATIC power in story-telling appears in several ways.
(*a*) In the first place the story, to resemble a drama, must
have a climax.

The Story of Joseph.

The story of Joseph owes much of its charm to the skill
with which the writer leads up to the climax,[2] in this case
the scene of recognition. Like a true artist he also reserves
the very simplest and most direct language for this moving
and critical part of the narrative.

The climax is delayed while Joseph mystifies and punishes
his brethren, insists on the coming of Benjamin, and when
Benjamin arrives threatens to detain him on suspicion of
theft. This constrains Judah to make his noble appeal, at
which Joseph breaks down and reveals himself. The appeal
is in the very simplest terms, a presentation of the case of the
brothers as clear as it is moving, a pathetic restatement of
the previous happenings :

> 'And thy servant my father said unto us, Ye know that my
> wife bare me two sons : and the one went out from me, and
> I said, Surely he is torn in pieces; and I have not seen him
> since : and if ye take this one also from me, and mischief befall
> him, ye shall bring down my gray hairs with sorrow to the
> grave.
> Now therefore when I come to thy servant my father, and the

[1] This lesson is short, to allow time for the compositions set for preparation to be discussed in class.

[2] The effectiveness of this climax is well described in Chaytor's *Story of
Israel and Judah*, p. 25.

lad be not with us; seeing that his life is bound up in the lad's life, it shall come to pass, when he seeth that the lad is not with us, that he will die: and thy servants shall bring down the gray hairs of thy servant our father with sorrow to the grave.

For thy servant became surety for the lad unto my father, saying, If I bring him not unto thee, then shall I bear the blame to my father for ever. Now therefore let thy servant, I pray thee, abide instead of the lad a bondman to my lord: and let the lad go up with his brethren. For how shall I go up to my father, and the lad be not with me? lest I see the evil that shall come on my father.'

It is all dignified, even for a suitor to the great Egyptian minister, and the language is extraordinarily simple and clear. The reply of Joseph is just as simple and direct:

'I am Joseph. Doth my father yet live?'

An inferior story-teller might have been tempted to spoil this climax by putting a long speech in the mouth of Joseph, but this is more natural. So is the effect upon the brothers natural. They 'could not answer him; for they were troubled at his presence'. And Joseph has to repeat his words.

Absalom's Death.

Another story with an equally good climax is that of the revolt of Absalom from David (2 Sam. xviii). The reporting of the catastrophe to the king is done with great skill.

First we are taken to the scene of battle, and see the two messengers starting, and one outstripping the other. Then we are taken to where David is, and wait with him for the runners' approach. He takes his seat at the gate. A watch-man mounting to the roof and scanning the plain (v. 24) fixes our attention. A solitary runner comes in sight. The watch-man calls the porter to look, and discusses the runners with David. The first runner, Ahimaaz, calls out 'Peace' from a distance, in keeping with his impetuous character (see his dialogue with Joab, vv. 19–23), but he keeps back the news of Absalom's death, and David is left in suspense, till the Cushite comes, and we who know the end wait anxiously for the blow to fall. When the Cushite has to face the question,

he nobly but vainly tries to break the shock by a little
oriental indirectness.[1]   But notice how the very simplicity of
the words chosen makes the tidings only the more solemn
and impressive:

> 'The enemies of my lord the king, and all that rise up against
> thee to do thee hurt, *be as that young man is*.'

In this way the bringing of the news is properly 'staged' by
a real artist in story-telling, who works up his details to
a climax, and chooses his words for the dramatic moment
with exquisite propriety.

Jehu's Revolt.

(*b*) The story of Jehu's revolt is dramatic for other reasons,
for the suddenness with which it is launched, and the speed
with which it moves (2 Kings ix).

Jehu is a man of quick and decisive action.   The key to
his character lies in the single sentence, 'for he driveth
furiously' (v. 21).   This is the only direct description of
Jehu, but the rapidity of the narrative with its abrupt action
and brusque dialogue gives a wonderful portrait of the
central figure and of his lightning revolt.   The story has
been called a 'photographic picture', and it might be transferred almost as it stands, dialogue and all, to a cinema film.

Note

(1) how brief the parley is at v. 13.

(2) Jehu's laconic answers and brusque questions, which
increase the impression of haste and decision, 'What
hast thou to do with peace?' he says twice to the messengers, 'Turn thee behind me'.   'What peace, so long as
the whoredoms of thy mother Jezebel and her witchcrafts
are so many?' he retorts to Joram.   Jezebel receives
no answer at all.   Argument is brushed aside.   'Who is
on my side, Who?' he calls up to the window.   If his
speed is terrible, so are his brief commands.   'Smite

[1] The oriental tactfulness here reminds us of the reply of the native to
the English nabob, whose son had been out shooting with no success: 'The
Sahib shot divinely but Providence was merciful to the birds.'

him also in his chariot.' ' Take him alive.' 'Go in and
slay them. Let none come forth.' A terrible captain !

(3) The part played by the watchman. A sentinel on a
tower gazing over a plain is a vivid figure in himself. In
this story and the last one about Absalom he serves to
extend the use of dialogue. The dramatic effect of the
dialogue will be obvious. Much of the excitement and
fascination of these incidents is due to the introduction of
this actor the watchman. If you eliminate the watchman
on the tower of Jezreel, and let the journey of Jehu be
reported in the third person, the life of the story goes.
As it is we use the watchman's eyes and hang upon his
words, see the horses galloping over the plain, and the
scouts of Joram meeting them in the distance. Those
who have read Homer will remember how he uses the
dialogue of Helen and Priam on the walls of Troy, while
Helen points out the various Greek heroes to the king, in
order to make their description more vivid.

Exercise. Tell the story of Henry II and Thomas à Becket, using as much
as possible the diction and style of the Old Testament and with
the Hebrew brevity and vigour.

Preparation (for lesson 4). Read 1 Kings xvii-2 Kings ii. Make a list of
the occasions on which Elijah intervened against the royal house,
and give the reasons for each intervention.

Lesson 4

DRAMATIC POWER (*continued*)

Elijah.

THE most dramatic story of all is that of Elijah.[1] Lively
and vigorous dialogue, sudden entrances and exits, the clash
of strong wills, scenes and characters that inspire fear and

---

[1] Mendelssohn dramatized it in his *Oratorio.*

pity, rapid action, climax, victory and defeat, all these are of
the drama, and all these will be found in the story of Elijah.

The personality of this prophet is generally admitted to be
the most dramatic in the Old Testament. His entrance into
the history is sudden, and the obscurity of his private life
only enhances the glamour of his public appearances. These
are rare and only occasioned by some sin of exceptional
magnitude committed by the reigning house. He comes to
denounce, and he departs on each occasion as abruptly as he
came.

The vigour and brevity of the dialogue are as remarkable
as in the story of Jehu. 'Art thou he that troubleth Israel ?'
'I have not troubled Israel, but thou and thy father's house
. . .'[1] 'Hast thou found me, O mine enemy?' 'I have
found thee, because thou hast sold thyself to do that which
is evil . . .'[2] 'How long halt ye between two opinions ? If
the Lord be God, follow him ; but if Baal, then follow him.'[3]
The commands flash out in the same dramatic way. 'Take
the prophets of Baal, let not one of them escape',[4] only
matched by the conciseness of Jezebel's threat.[5]

Elijah's will clashes with Jezebel's as they fight for the
conscience of Ahab. The dramatic scenes are numerous, the
meeting, after the famine, between Elijah and Ahab, arranged
through Obadiah, the trial of fire on Mount Carmel, the
announcement of the rain, the revelation to Elijah in the
desert, the call of Elisha, and the ascension of Elijah.
Notice how the coming of the rain is announced. The
employment of the boy as messenger keeps up the suspense,
and the reader uses the boy's eyes, and the cloud is described
in direct speech. It is the same dramatic use of an additional
actor as the use of a watchman in the stories of Jehu and of
the death of Absalom. The scene on Mount Carmel is the
terrible climax, but the action moves rapidly, and failure
follows on the heels of triumph.

The scene on Mount Carmel is very vividly described, the

[1] 1 Kings xviii. 17.   [2] xxi. 20.   [3] xviii. 21.
[4] ibid. 40.   [5] xix. 2.

head of the new prophetic schools upholding the worship of Jehovah singlehanded against the priests of the foreign worship. The people are cowed spectators, and they answer to Elijah's challenge 'never a word'. The priests of Baal, having the pick of the animals, are compelled to go through their vain ceremony, and work themselves up into greater and greater frenzy, and arouse the irony of Elijah, pointed for the benefit of the people, for Jehovah never slept, 'He that keepeth Israel shall neither slumber nor sleep'. The frenzies die down at last, the priests retire, there seems to be a hush, the hush of the evening sacrifice, when softer and better feelings prevail, and the minds of the people would turn with relief from the vulgar scene which they had just witnessed in the glare of the noonday sun. Elijah has made the priests of Baal a generous allowance of time that their god might return from his hunting, and now, as though to brush aside the mummery which they had just witnessed, and force the apathetic people to take a more active interest, he says to them, 'Come near unto me'. He deliberately repairs the altar so long broken down, soaks the sacrifice to avoid suspicion of trickery, makes a step forward to the altar, and utters one brief, noble petition, '. . . Hear me, O Lord, hear me, that this people may know that thou, Lord, art God, and that thou hast turned their heart back again'. Then the fire falls and consumes the sacrifice and the wood and the stones and the dust, and licks up the water in the trench. This brings the people to their knees. Notice the effective repetition, 'The Lord, he is the God, the Lord, he is the God'. Elijah then makes them commit themselves by the slaughter of the priests, before the effect of their conversion should wear off.

The prayer for rain follows. Elijah's very attitude in prayer is described, and the appearance of the little cloud, also the act of homage to his lord the king performed by the prophet in his exhilaration as he runs before the royal chariot to Jezreel.

No less dramatic, though easily explicable, is Elijah's sudden panic. He 'had been drawing too much upon the

body, and in such cases nature repays herself from the
spirit '.[1]   The moral strain of the struggle on Mount Carmel
and the physical strain of the running to Jezreel, perhaps
after fasting, brought on a reaction, usual after such whirlwind displays of zeal.   He had taken public opinion by
storm, and he suddenly turns self-conscious.   He begins to
measure his own success, 'I have been very jealous for the
Lord, . . . I, even I, only am left . . .'   He reproaches God
for his undeserved fortune.   When food and rest have braced
him up, the conscience of the reformer reawakes.   'What
am I doing here ?   What of those loyal thousands to whom
I was supposed to be giving a lead ?'   His heart still surges
with the memory of his struggle, and demands comfort for his
apparent failure.   He buries himself in the mountain wilds.

Another vivid scene or tableau follows.   To comfort
Elijah's despairing heart, God plays on nature as on an
organ.   He cures like with like.   To satisfy the turbulent
emotions and disordered passions of the prophet's spirit,
God first lets nature sound her loudest with crashing
discords.   The prophet of wrath, Elijah, has passed through
earthquakes, fires, and storms, and peace is brought to him
by sympathy with the convulsions of nature.   When the
loudest stops of the organ have played their part, he has an
ear to hear the soft sounds of the 'voice celestial',[2] 'What
doest thou here, Elijah ?', and the still, small voice which
has become a by-word attuned his soul once more to his
God's own purposes.[3]

[1] T. R. Glover, *Conflict of Religions in the early Roman Empire*, p. 129,
in reference to Jesus on the Cross.

[2] Like the organ 'stop' called the 'voix céleste'.

[3] *Note.* The terms of Elijah's new commission contained still more
practical consolation.   The appointment of Elisha guarantees the con-
tinuance of his work, and the safety of the schools of the prophets, his
special care (see 2 Kings ii).   The revolt against the line of Ahab and its
doom are to be originated by the prophetic act of anointing, the traditional
privilege of the prophets from Samuel downwards, by which they set aside
kings who were disloyal to the national religion of Jehovah.   Finally
Elijah's pessimistic estimate of the numerical strength of the true worshippers
is gently corrected, 'Yet have I left me seven thousand in Israel . . .'

Everything Elijah does is dramatic. In calling Elisha to be prophet, he casts his mantle over him, as he follows the plough, and leaves him without a word. His action in 2 Kings i is like the rest. The final scene is a worthy close to the drama. Elijah impresses us so powerfully that one feels that artistic propriety, if nothing else, demands that he should not die like common men, but make a more dramatic exit. When he goes round to confirm the schools of prophets, to which he acted no doubt as an Archbishop to his clergy, the end is duly led up to by prophecies. 'Knowest thou that the Lord will take away thy master from thy head to-day?' And Elisha replied, 'Yea, I know it; hold ye your peace'. A new interest is given by the doubt whether Elisha will fully succeed to Elijah's powers. Elisha's great outcry closes the drama, 'My father, my father, the chariots of Israel and the horsemen thereof'. And he saw him no more.

Exercise. In what respects are Elisha's character and story less dramatic than those of Elijah?

Preparation (for lesson 5). Read the story of Jonah.

Lesson 5

PARABLE

The Story of Jonah.

MENTION has already been made of the love of stories which the Jews shared with other Eastern peoples, and which led them to prefer short memoirs of great men to connected and regular history. Besides these stories of historical personalities the writers of the Old Testament used the story for teaching great truths, that is by way of parable, preferring illustration to argument, and the concrete and personal to abstract proposition. So the garden of Eden and the serpent are still remembered and grip the simplest imagination, and the parables of Christ survive the sermons preached upon them. Perhaps the Eastern mind would not understand the passion of the Western child for asking at the end of a story, Is it true? A higher truth may often be taught from a story of the imagination than from the facts of history.

Such a story is the book of Jonah, but it differs from the parables of Jesus in that it is narrated about a historical personage who lived some centuries before the writer's time, and is mentioned in 2 Kings xiv. 25. Unfortunately the incident of the whale, much misunderstood, and the curious controversy that was waged about the literal truth of the story, diverted readers' attention from its literary merits as from the wonderful lesson it conveys, so that it may not be out of place to give special prominence to them here.

The literary merits of the story are again its simplicity of diction, its absence of superfluous detail, its rapid movement (note especially ch. i, vv. 4–6, 15, 16), its vivid use of dialogue, but above all the dramatic way in which the characters of the persons are expressed in the action, so that the moral of the book is brought out as much by what they do, as by the gentle remonstrance of Jehovah, which itself is perfect in its brevity. In a word the literary value of the book cannot be fully appreciated apart from its artistic treatment as a parable.

In the fifth century B.C. when the writer lived, the feeling of the Jews against the world around them had hardened and become embittered. Instead of believing with the prophets that their nation was to be 'a light to the Gentiles', they were hoping to see the Gentile races destroyed for the vindication of their own nation. Jonah in the story represents this attitude and stands for Israel, and the lesson taught to Jonah was a parable to his descendants. That lesson was that even the heathen had a place in God's purpose and were precious in his sight. Their sins were due to ignorance which deserved pity. The writer is preaching to the exclusive Jew a lesson of tolerance and charity.

Points in the story that enforce this lesson and are of literary interest are as follow:

CHAPTER I.

v. 2 Nineveh is selected as the most hated heathen city. As it was destroyed in 607 B.C., it is obviously taken as a type, not literally and historically. Note how it is drawn in a couple of strokes, 'that great city', 'their wickedness is come up before me', and the drama begins at once.

3 Cf. v. 12. Jonah tries to flee from the presence of the Lord, as though he was the God of one place only. Yet he believed in him as the Creator, v. 9, and as able to save or destroy Nineveh. So the restored Jews tended to regard Jehovah as confined to Jerusalem.

4 A single verse is enough to describe the storm, the next rapidly contrasts the fear and hasty action of the sailors with the negligence of Jonah. The diction of the original Hebrew is vivid, personifying the ship, 'The

ship *thought to be broken*', i. e. 'thought it would be broken'.

5–16 The character of the sailors as heathen is kindly and sympathetically drawn. Though less enlightened than Jonah, they in a sense convert him by their unselfishness and piety :

   i. they go to their prayers, when the storm arises, and are shocked that Jonah neglects to do so (v. 6).

   ii. they sacrifice their goods to save the ship before approaching the stranger (v. 5).

   iii. try to save him contrary to his own advice (v. 13).

   iv. ask Jehovah (Jonah's God) to absolve them from the guilt of shedding innocent blood (v. 14).

   v. readily believe in Jehovah (v. 16).

  13 The diction is again expressive and vigorous, 'the men *dug* the sea', 'the sea wrought and was tempestuous' (A. V.).

CHAPTER III.

5–9 The readiness of the Ninevites to hear and repent is shown.

  2 'Was not this my saying . . . ? Therefore I hasted to flee . . .' shows the temper of Jonah, and of the race which he represents ; he had run away because he felt God would spare the hated Gentile ; yet mercy was the ancient attribute of Jehovah, which the Jews were ignoring.

  5 He still lingers near in the hope the city may perish.

9–10 Show Jonah tender towards the gourd, though ruthless towards Nineveh. His tenderness was selfish, in so far as the gourd sheltered him, but in v. 10 it is suggested the pity was also partly unselfish. He had grown interested in it and pitied its untimely death. The lesson is then driven home ; if Jonah had sympathy with a gourd, which grew without his care, had sprung up at short notice, and was only of temporary interest to him, what should God feel towards a great city, with a great history, and its great multitude of souls, over whom he had watched so long, and who could not 'discern between their right hand and their left'.

11 'and also much cattle'. Cf. the Psalmists, Ps. civ, &c. Even on these, much more on human beings, God has pity.

It is noticeable that this breadth of mind and view, shared by Jeremiah and 2 Isaiah, did not find much response until Judaism was transformed by Christianity.

The Fish.

If the meaning of the book be taken as suggested by modern scholars, the incident of the fish is of comparative unimportance. But Jonah swallowed and disgorged by the fish corresponds to the swallowing of Judaea by Babylon and the release of the Exiles. Compare Jer. li. 34, 44, where the king of Babylon swallows Israel like a dragon, and is to disgorge him at God's bidding.

The ode in chapter ii. is thought to be a later addition to the book.[1]

Exercise.　i. Summarize the contents of the book of Daniel, chap. i–vi.
The rest of the book is what is called Apocalyptic literature, i.e. literature that claims to reveal the future, or the unseen, the writer despairing of the age he lives in and seeking comfort for his countrymen from the deliverance which 'the day of the Lord' will bring in the distant future. The book of Daniel was written about 165 B.C., to encourage the Jews to resist Antiochus and his sacrileges, just as Revelation in the New Testament was to encourage the Christians under their persecutions with the hope of the Millennium.
ii. Compare the second part of Daniel with the Book of Revelation, pointing out any similarity of subject-matter.

Preparation (for lesson 6). Read the following passages with a view to comparing them later ; Gen. xxviii. 10–22, Exod. iii. 1–7, xxxiii. 12–xxxiv. 9, 1 Kings xix. 8–18, Job xxxviii. 1 ff., Isa. vi. 1–9.

Note. The above account is based on that of G. Adam Smith, *The Twelve Prophets*, where additional details and fuller explanations may be found.

Lesson 6

The APPEARANCES of GOD

THE epithet most commonly applied to the style of the Old Testament is the epithet 'sublime'. It is particularly applicable to certain passages in the narrative which may be classed by themselves, the so-called 'theophanies', or appearances of God revealing himself to his chosen servants. These are by writers who belonged to different times and schools of thought, but in most of them the supernatural is treated in the same way, with restraint and dignity, and it is presented by a uniform method, which is worth analysis.

All attempts to describe God or divine processes must of course fail. The desire to see God has produced grotesque idolatry. Even the intellectual Greeks satisfied themselves to some extent by representing gods in human shape. As the witty Frenchman said, 'God made man in his own image, and man has been returning the compliment ever since'. What these passages in the Old Testament succeed in doing is to suggest to the reader in a remarkable way the *presence* of God. They come nearer to satisfying our imagination or what a divine revelation must be like than any other human account before Christianity has done.

The Jewish leaders steadily refused to allow pictures or images. The people had at various times satisfied themselves with 'calves' as symbols. To worship a god without visible form was small comfort to them. The prophets therefore used the utmost resources of language to make them feel more really the divine majesty and goodness. The earlier narratives, as has already been pointed out, use phrases which give to God human habits and almost human shape. 'God walked in the garden in the cool of the day.' The creation of woman in the second chapter of Genesis is conceived in a similar vein; 'God took one of his (Adam's) ribs and closed up the flesh thereof, and the rib . . . made he woman.' But the first words of Genesis, which come from a later writer, are in a very different strain, and are selected by the great critic Longinus as one of the sublimest expressions of divine power: 'God said, Let there be light, and there was light.' In this account of creation in Genesis i. there are no childish stories of eggs and hatchings of matter as in other ancient theologies. The writer merely suggests the strength and majesty of the creative presence. 'The spirit of God moved (or 'was brooding') upon the face of the waters.'

The passages referred to above, the theophanies, while showing a similar restraint, leave a wonderful impression of divinity upon the mind. Among the chief passages we may put the following:

(1) Jacob's vision at Bethel
(2) the revelation to Moses in the bush
(3) the revelation to Moses on Mount Sinai
(4) the revelation to Elijah on Mount Horeb
(5) the answer of God to Job
(6) the vision of Isaiah.

In these there are four common features:

i. Some natural phenomenon such as a whirlwind as the sign of God's presence, or a cloud as the cloak or veil drawn over it.

ii. a voice declaring some aspect or quality of God.

iii. some expression or action of the servant, who receives the revelation, which may suggest dreadful mystery.

iv. some definite purpose of the revelation, of bringing comfort or confirmation to the servant in question.

Passage.	Name of servant.	Natural phenomenon.	The Voice's declaration.	The Mystery.	Purpose.
Gen. xxviii. 10-22.	Jacob.	Light in the form of a staircase from earth to heaven.	'I am the Lord God of Abraham,' i. e. God is the God of his fathers.	'Surely the Lord is in this place . . . how dreadful is this place.'	Comfort to the exile and confirmation to him of the family blessing.
[1] Exod. iii. 1-7.	Moses.	Bush on fire without burning.	'I am that I am.' 'I AM hath sent me unto you.' Eternity of God.	'Put off thy shoes . . . for the place is holy.' And Moses hid his face.	Commission given to Moses.
[1] Exod. xxxiii. 12- xxxiv. 9.	Moses.	The Lord descended *in the cloud.*	'The Lord, the Lord, a God full of compassion and mercy.'	And Moses made haste and bowed his head and worshipped.	God's presence promised to Moses.
1 Kings xix. 8-18.	Elijah.	A great and strong wind, . . . an earthquake, . . . a fire.	'A still, small voice,' (Heb. 'a sound of gentle stillness), . . . 'What doest thou here, Elijah ?'	He wrapped his face in his mantle.	Comfort of Elijah and a new commission.
Job xxxviii. 1 ff.	Job.	Whirlwind.	God's recital of the wonders of nature. (Optimism 'leaks out of God's reply,' says Chesterton.)	'Now mine eye seeth thee, wherefore I abhor myself and repent in dust and ashes.'	Consolation of Job.

[1] There is a difference between these appearances to Moses and that to the elders in Exod. xxiv. 11. Here God's face is too terrible to be looked upon by men, there it is said that the elders 'beheld' God, and were not harmed. Also the description of God's throne is there attempted, something after the manner of Ezekiel's attempts, which are too ambitious.

Passage.	Name of servant.	Natural phenomenon.	The Voice's declaration.	The Mystery.	Purpose.
Isa. vi. 1–9.	Isaiah.	Earthquake and smoke.	'Holy, holy, holy, is the Lord of Hosts.'	The seraphim veil their faces before God. Isaiah says, 'I am undone, for mine eyes have seen the King, the Lord of Hosts.'	Purification of Isaiah and a commission given to him.

Some of these passages are among the most sublime in the Old Testament. Notice

(1) the atmosphere of awe and mystery produced by the natural phenomena, and their effect upon the seer in each case, e. g. 'he wrapped his face in his mantle'.

The actual appearance of God is always veiled in obscurity, or is, as Milton says, 'dark with the excess of light', not as in the most primitive accounts, to which reference has been made. Burke[1] in his treatise on the sublime quotes the following passage from Job to show how this obscurity increases the solemnity and terror that accompany the vision :

'In thoughts from the visions of the night, when deep sleep falleth upon men, fear came upon me and trembling, which made all my bones to shake. Then a spirit passed before my face, the hair of my flesh stood up ; it stood still, but I could not discern the appearance thereof ; a form was before my eyes ; there was silence and I heard a voice, "Shall mortal man be more just than God ?" ' (iv. 13–16).

'Notice', says Burke, 'that when the grand cause of the terror appears, it is wrapped up in incomprehensible darkness, more awful than the liveliest description could have made it.'

(2) The striking declarations of the Voice, 'I AM', the simplest possible description of God's eternity, 'Holy, holy, holy, is the Lord of Hosts,' 'The Lord, the Lord God gracious and merciful', and again the sublime review of all

[1] *The Sublime and Beautiful*, Part II, 4.

the wonderful and terrible things in nature, which convinces Job, without answering all his questions, because, as Mr. Chesterton says, 'he feels the terrible and tingling atmosphere of something which is too good to be told.'[1] Jacob at Bethel is similarly impressed. Lonely and sinking in heart, when he fell asleep, he wakes to a sense of majesty and awe. 'This is none other but the house of God, and this is the gate of Heaven.' Most sublime of all perhaps is the scene on Mount Horeb, and yet the phenomena that accompany the revelation are purely natural phenomena:

> 'And, behold, the Lord passed by, and a great and strong wind rent the mountains, and brake in pieces the rocks before the Lord; but the Lord was not in the wind: and after the wind an earthquake, but the Lord was not in the earthquake: and after the earthquake a fire, but the Lord was not in the fire: and after the fire a still small voice. And it was so, when Elijah heard it, that he wrapped his face in his mantle, and went out, and stood in the entering in of the cave. And, behold, there came a voice unto him, and said, What doest thou here, Elijah?'

Exercise. Examine the vision in Ezek. i. 26 ff. Compare it with those in Isa. vi and in Exod. xxxiii. 12–xxxiv. 9. In what respects is it inferior?

Preparation (for lesson 6). i. Collect all the similes in the prophet Amos, and show how they reflect his calling as a herdsman. Quote further similes from the Old Testament which reflect the pastoral habits of the Hebrews.

ii. Read Amos iii, and explain fully the comparison made in vv. 3–8.

[1] Commenting on Job xxxviii. 4–7, 'Where wast thou when I laid the foundations of the earth? . . . when the morning stars sang together and all the sons of God shouted for joy?' Mr. Chesterton says 'they must have had something to sing and shout for.'

Lesson 7

The POETRY *of the* OLD TESTAMENT

BEAUTY in poetry is not easy to analyse, but Hebrew poetry has certain prominent features, belonging both to its lyrics, like the Psalms, and also to the prophetical books, which are nearer to poetry than to prose. Further, since Hebrew poetry does not employ rhyme, but balances thought rather than sound, one of the difficulties of translation did not occur, and it is possible to appreciate the poetry in an English version more easily perhaps than that of other foreign literatures.

The *style* of Hebrew poetry presents the following chief features :

1. Wonderful imagery, including simile, metaphor, and allegory,
2. a striking use of literary figures and devices, as personification, hyperbole (intentional exaggeration), rhetorical questions,
3. irony,
4. balance or parallelism of thought,
5. a concise and vigorous diction,
6. beauty of rhythm.

The last two can only be properly appreciated in the original Hebrew, but the genius of the English translators has gone far to compensate the loss in the authorized version.

The *thought* of Hebrew poetry, on the other hand, is concentrated upon one dominant idea—God, and man's relation to God. To express this idea is the aim of all the literary devices mentioned above. The Hebrew prophet, trying to explain Jehovah to his pagan audience, says almost despairingly, 'What is God like, and unto what will ye liken him?' Their answer took the form of idols, his was given by comparisons or similes, by metaphors and allegories, drawn either from the wonders of nature and creation, from fire or light or human relationships, or from the great things God had done for his people in the past. The variety, beauty, and dignity of this imagery is the glory of the literature of the Old Testament.

When we try to put all these images or pictures into one, as they appear in the Psalms or Isaiah, we have a vivid impression of the Jewish Jehovah, a terrible God of righteousness softening into the God of mercy, the Father of the New Testament. As the Creator, he 'stretches out the heavens like a curtain', and 'measures the universe with a span'. 'The mountains melt at his presence', 'the nations are as nothing before him.' His resources are so vast that he could afford to make such apparently useless creatures as the wild beasts. Yet, as the wonderful nature Psalms tell us, though his great hand made the terrible mammoth and the whale, his gentle eye also watches over the feeding of the young ravens, and provides homes for the coney and the stork. 'He feeds his flock like a shepherd and carries the lambs in his bosom.' His flock is primarily the Israelites, troubled and scattered by their enemies for a time, but soon to be gathered up and restored. All the world will benefit by that restoration. The servant of Jehovah, who is to restore his chosen people, will also be a 'light to lighten the Gentiles', and 'kings and nations shall come to that light', the whole creation shall be at peace, and sorrow and sighing shall flee away. For 'the everlasting God, the Creator of the ends of the earth, fainteth not', and as he can number even all the hosts of the stars, and calls them by their names, so the fortunes of the sons of Jacob are not hid from him, and 'if they wait upon the Lord they shall renew their strength,

they shall mount up with wings as eagles, they shall run and
not be weary, they shall walk and not faint.'

Note. Snatches of song and lyrical odes are printed as verse in the
revised version and are more easily recognized as poetry. Blessings and
curses are usually in verse, see Gen. iv. 23, 24, xxvii. 27–29, 39, 40,
xlix. 2–27.

Similes.

Types of simile in the Old Testament:

(*a*) grotesque—

'Remember, I beseech thee, that thou hast fashioned me as
clay. Hast thou not *poured me out as milk and curdled me like
cheese?*' Job x. 10.

(Contrast the far greater mystery and solemnity of the language of Ps. cxxxix. 13–16, on the same subject).

(*b*) homely but forcible—

'God shall *wipe* Jerusalem *as a dish, turning it upside down.*'
2 Kings xxi. 13.

'Now shall this multitude *lick up* all that is round about us,
as the ox licketh up the grass of the field.' Num. xxii. 4.

More striking still is the one which illustrated the spoliations
of the terrible Assyrian:

'My hand hath found *as a nest* the riches of the peoples; and
as one gathereth eggs that are forsaken, have I gathered all the
earth, and there was none that *moved the wing, or that opened the
mouth or chirped.*' Isa. x. 14.

(*c*) picturesque—

'The children of Israel encamped before them *like two little
flocks of kids.*' 1 Kings xx. 27.

(*d*) beautiful—

'He shall be *as rivers of water in a dry place, as the shadow of
a great rock in a weary land.*' Isa. xxxii. 2.

The imagery of the Old Testament includes similes, metaphors, allegory, and parables, all used in great abundance.
There are certain peculiarities in the Hebrew use of these
figures, and these peculiarities are common to most of the
Hebrew poets and prophets, though of course the various
writers have their own individual styles.

The Similes are invariably short:

'As the hart panteth after the water brooks, so panteth my soul after thee, O God.' Ps. xlii. 1.

If the comparison is pursued, the simile passes into metaphor:

'My soul *thirsteth* for God, for the living God.' Ps. xlii. 2.

'Judah is a lion's whelp; *from the prey*, my son, *thou art gone up.*' Gen. xlix. 9.

The classical poets, Roman and Greek, elaborate their similes into complete pictures. The countless stars, for example, are often used as an illustration in the Old Testament, 'As the hosts of heaven cannot be numbered, so will I multiply the seed of David' (Jer. xxxiii. 22). Homer works up this illustration into a beautiful landscape scene:

'Even as when in heaven the stars above the bright moon shine clear to see, when the air is windless and all the peaks appear, and the tall headlands and glades and all the stars are seen, and the shepherd's heart is glad, even in like multitude appeared the watchfires.' *Iliad*, viii. 555 ff.

Here, after the simple comparison, the poet lingers to finish the picture in his mind, which would not have interested the Hebrew, wholly absorbed in his religious problems and message.[1] The nearest approach to this in form and in length is the well-known analogy in the song of Moses from an eagle training its young to fly, used to illustrate God's training of the children of Israel:

'As an eagle that stirreth up her nest, that fluttereth over her young, spreadeth abroad her wings, taketh them, beareth them on her wings: the Lord alone did lead him.' Deut. xxxii. 11 f.

Even this simile is wonderfully condensed; the eagle, according to some observant travellers, scatters with its feet the sticks of the nest when she wishes her young to learn to fly, then flutters over them, as they tremble on the ledge of rock, persuading them to try their wings, and as they lose their nerve and are falling, flies under them and bears them up on her outspread pinions. So the young nation of Israel in the

[1] For other examples see the end of this section.

wilderness was trained to feel its feet, as it were, under
God's eye.

But the Hebrew custom in using the pure simile is to give
a rapid series of short comparisons:

> 'O, my God, make them *like the whirling dust, as stubble before
> the wind, as the fire that burneth the forest*, and *as the flame that
> setteth the mountains on fire.*' Ps. lxxxiii. 13.

> 'My days are swifter *than a post* . . . they are passed away *as
> the swift ships, as the eagle that swoopeth on the prey.*' Job ix. 25.

The effect is to give a wonderful vigour and vividness to the
style. It is not uncommon to find the simile transposed into
a question:

> 'Can a woman forget her child? Yet will I not forget thee?'

Amos the prophet produces a powerful effect by a rapid
series of such questions, leading up to a climax in true
oratorical style. See Amos iii. 1–8.

The variety of these short similes is immense. Some idea
is obtained by collecting those only which illustrate the transitoriness of human life. Men are as grass,[1] as a flower,[2] as
a shadow,[2] as grass upon the housetops,[3] which withereth
before it groweth up; they waste away like the waters of the
sea and river.[4] Their houses are houses of clay, which are
crushed before the moth.[5] Their days are swifter than a
weaver's shuttle,[6] like the cloud vanishing away,[7] like swift
ships,[8] swifter than a post,[8] swift as the eagle that swoopeth
on the prey,[8] carried away as with a flood, as a sleep, as a watch
in the night;[9] their 'tent-cord is plucked up'.[10] The wicked
are as a green tree, which suddenly disappears.[11] Judah's
goodness is as a morning cloud, and as the dew that goeth
early away.[12] The annihilation of the Assyrians is like the
sudden disappearance of the grasshoppers, which 'camp in
the hedges in the cold day, but when the sun ariseth, they
flee away'.[13]

---

[1] Ps. ciii. 15.   [2] Job xiv. 2.   [3] Ps. cxxix. 6.
[4] Job xiv. 11.   [5] Ibid., iv. 19.   [6] Ibid., vii. 6.
[7] Ibid., vii. 9.   [8] Ibid., ix. 25.   [9] Ps. xc. 4.   [10] Job iv. 21.
[11] Ps. xxxvii. 35.   [12] Hosea vi. 4.   [13] Nahum iii. 17.

With this transitoriness God's permanence is contrasted in a great variety of well-known similes, such as the rock, the high tower, the strong mountains, though even these bow and melt before him.

Note. Homeric similes (see above, p. 53).

Compare the simile used by Achilles:

> 'Wherefore weepest thou, Patroclus, like a fond little maid, that runs by her mother's side, and bids her mother take her up, snatching at her gown, and hinders her going, and tearfully looks up at her, till the mother takes her up? *Iliad*, xiv. 7–10.

Or the beautiful one of the nightingale in Vergil's fourth Georgic:

> 'As the nightingale wailing in the poplar shade plains for her lost young, that the rustic churl with his prying eye has taken unfledged from the nest; while she weeps the night through, and sitting on a branch, renews her piteous melody, and fills the country round with the plaints of her sorrow,' *Georg.* iv. 511–16 (Conington).

There are many details in these similes which help to complete a picture but are not essential to the comparison. A still longer and even more beautiful simile is M. Arnold's of the eagle in *Sohrab and Rustum*, ll. 536 ff.:

> As when some hunter in the spring hath found
> A breeding eagle sitting on her young . . .

An interesting section on Homeric similes has lately appeared in Drinkwater's *Outlines of Literature*, published in fortnightly parts.

Preparation (for lesson 8). Define the term allegory. Illustrate it by Bunyan's *Pilgrim's Progress*. Explain the allegory there in detail.

Read Psalm lxxx.

Lesson 8

ALLEGORIES

THE poetry and the prophetic books of the Old Testament are full of short similes, illustrating some single idea, such as the transitoriness of human life, as already mentioned. When the short simile was not sufficient, when the writer wished to compare a real and an imaginary set of circumstances, instead of using the classical simile, he either plunged into metaphor, as we have seen (p. 53), or used a specially vivid form of allegory. This vivid effect he produced by skilfully interweaving the figurative language with the literal facts, mixing the real and the allegorical. The hard facts show through the veil of allegory, which softens and beautifies them.

A notable example is in Psalm lxxx, where the cruel fate of Palestine is compared with that of a ravaged vine.

1 Give ear, O Shepherd of Israel,
Thou that leadest Joseph like a flock;
Thou that sittest upon the cherubim,
shine forth.
2 Before Ephraim, and Benjamin, and
Manasseh, stir up thy might, and come
to save us.
3 Turn us again, O God; and cause thy
face to shine, and we shall be saved.

The refrain. See also vv. 7, 14, 19.

4 O Lord God of hosts, how long wilt
thou be angry against the prayer of thy
people?
5 Thou hast fed them with the bread of
tears, and given them tears to drink in
large measure.
6 Thou makest us a strife unto our
neighbours: and our enemies laugh
among themselves.
7 Turn us again, O God of hosts; and
cause thy face to shine, and we shall
be saved.

The Allegory.

8 Thou broughtest a vine out of Egypt:[1]
Thou didst drive out the nations,[2] and
plantedst it.
9 Thou preparedst room before it,
And it took deep root and filled the
land.
10 The mountains[3] were covered with the
shadow of it,
And the boughs thereof were like the
cedars of God.
11 She sent out her branches unto the sea,[4]
And her shoots unto the River.[4]

[1] The migration, as in Exodus.
[2] The Canaanites, see Joshua.

[3] The highest part of Palestine was occupied by the Israelites, the Philistines holding the plains.
[4] The Mediterranean ... the Jordan.

12 Why hast thou broken down her fences,[1]
   So that all they which pass by the way do pluck her?
13 The boar out of the wood doth ravage it,
   And the wild beasts of the field feed on it.

14 Turn again, we beseech thee, O God of hosts,[2]
   Look down from heaven, and behold, and visit this vine.
15 And the stock which thy right hand hath planted,
   And the branch that thou madest strong for thyself.
16 It is burned with fire, it is cut down:
   They perish at the rebuke of thy countenance.
17 Let thy hand be upon the man of thy right hand,
   Upon the son of man whom thou madest strong for thyself.
18 So shall we not go back from thee:
   quicken thou us and we will call upon thy name.

19 Turn us again, O Lord God of hosts;
   Cause thy face to shine, and we shall be saved.

[1] Through Palestine lay the main route between Egypt and Assyria, whose kings broke down its 'fenced' cities on their way to attack one another (the 'boar' and the 'wild beast').

[2] Notice here how naturally the speaker turns from the allegory to the personal misfortune, yet retains the image. The Hebrew has 'son', thinking of Israel and dropping the allegory for a moment, as in v. 17.

Compare with v. 15 and note the skilful variation.

The beautiful refrain to close.

It will be noticed how the special features of Palestine, its river, the sea, its hills and cedars, are preserved in the allegory, and how the growth of the vine is a picture of the spread of the Israelites over the land, when they came up into it out of Egypt. Jesus, in the same way, gave a touch of realism to his parable of the Good Samaritan by the opening words, ' A certain man went down *from Jerusalem to Jericho*', a road well known to his hearers as the scene of robberies. The effect of the refrain is striking, breaking into the allegory, and keeping the real tragedy uppermost throughout (especially at ver. 14).

Other things contribute to the beauty of this lyric, which are referred to in a later chapter, e. g.

   i. the parallelism, or balance of the verses.

   ii. the imagery, as in ver. 1, the simile of the *shepherd*, the image 'that *sittest upon the cherubim*', the metaphors again in v. 3, '*cause thy face to shine*', and in v. 5, '*the bread of tears*'.

iii. the sudden question in v. 12,

but in the main the singular pathos of the appeal is due to the skilful use of allegory.

Exercise. Read Ezek. xix. 10–14, and compare the similar allegory there with that of the Psalmist, (*a*) in matter, (*b*) in literary charm.

Personification

While the Hebrew did not believe in river-gods, he personified nature for literary purposes. Any part of nature may be regarded as God's agent, and responds to the touch of his hand. Thus 'the sun rejoiceth as a strong man to run his course',[1] in order to declare the glory of God. The heavens are bidden to *sing in sympathy* with God's word, 'for the Lord hath done it'.[2]

Personification consists in the Old Testament mostly of that kind which attributes feelings to inanimate things. 'Shout, ye lower parts of the earth; break forth into singing, ye mountains, O forest, and every tree therein, for the Lord hath redeemed Jacob, and will glorify himself in Israel'.[3] The pestilence *marches* before Jehovah when he comes to battle, and the sea, as he passes, *lifts up his hands on high.*[4] What to the pagan mind was a real superstition, to the Hebrew is a mere figure of speech. These majestic per-

---

[1] Ps. xix. 5, 6.
[2] Isa. xlix. 13.
[3] Ibid., xliv. 23.
[4] Hab. iii. 5, 10.

sonifications are always occurring: Hades *extends her throat*
and *opens her jaws* to receive the rich fools[1]; Wisdom was
'with God in the beginning as a master workman', and speaks
for herself.[2] What solemnity personification gives to the
inquiry concerning wisdom in Job:

> 'The deep saith, It is not in me,
> And the sea saith, It is not with me.
> Destruction and death say, We have heard a rumour thereof
> with our ears.'[3]

Jerusalem is addressed as a virgin:

> 'Awake, awake, put on thy strength, O Zion;
> Put on thy beautiful garments, O Jerusalem.'[4]

The style at once becomes animated and dramatic.[5]

Hyperbole.

Hyperbole, as a literary figure, is an intentional exaggeration, by which a speaker obviously overstates his case and
yet carries greater conviction. The hearer is aware of the
exaggeration, but provided it be conveyed in a novel or
striking manner, he is impressed in spite of himself. American
humour owes much of its effect to hyperbole, as Scotch
humour relies rather on understatement. Outside the sphere
of humour hyperboles are the peculiar property of orators.
The most picturesque piece of oratory in the Bible is that of
Hushai the Archite, by which he induced Absalom not to
pursue David. As the orator warms to his theme, he
exaggerates more and more:

> [6]'Thou knowest thy father and his men, that they be mighty
> men, and they be chafed in their minds, *as a bear robbed of her*

[1] Isa. v. 14.   [2] Prov. viii. 30.
[3] Job xxviii. 14, 22.   [4] Isa. lii. 1.
[5] For the different kinds of personification see the examples given in
Abbott's *English Lessons*, pp. 131–134.
[6] The first similes used are merely 'flowery'. The hyperboles are
printed in heavy type.

whelps in the field. . . . When some of them (Absalom's men) be
fallen, . . . whosoever heareth it, will say, " There is a slaughter
among the people that follow Absalom." And even he that is
valiant, whose heart is *as the heart of a lion*, shall **utterly melt**. . . .
But I counsel that all Israel be gathered together unto thee . . .
as the sand that is by the sea for multitude, and that thou go
to battle in thine own person. So shall we come upon him in
some place where he shall be found, and will **light upon him,
as the dew falleth on the ground,** and of him and of all the
men that are with him we will **not leave so much as one.**
Moreover, if he be gotten into a city, then shall all Israel **bring
ropes to that city, and we will draw it into the river, until
there be not one small stone found there.'** [1]

There is a real crescendo of boasting here, it will be noticed,
culminating in the absurd threat at the end.

Other hyperboles of a similar type are those used by
Moses threatening Pharaoh :

'Against any of the children of Israel **shall not a dog move
his tongue,'** [2]

or addressing the rebellious Israelites themselves :

'As for them that are left of you, I will send a faintness into
their heart in the lands of their enemies, and **the sound of a
driven leaf shall chase them.'** [3]

Another is put into the mouth of the Assyrian :

'With the sole of my feet **will I dry up all the rivers of
Egypt,'** [4]

referring to the multitudes of his army, for whose drink, as
some interpret it, the water of the Nile would not suffice.

Another type of hyperbole merges in personification :

'**The sun and moon stood still** at the light of thine arrows.' [5]

This is much more vivid and striking than if the prophet had
said, that the sun and moon were eclipsed by God's lightnings.

---

[1] 2 Sam. xvii. 8–14.   [2] Exod. xi. 7.   [3] Lev. xxvi. 36.
[4] Isa. xxxvii. 25.   [5] Hab. iii. 11.

Some hyperboles, literally untrue, may really fall short of truth, just as the expression used by Jesus, 'the very hairs of your head *are all numbered*', whilst not, of course, meaning that an actual account is kept, only faintly suggests the infinite watchfulness of Providence. Compare the account of the new Jerusalem in Isaiah (liv. 11, 12).

Preparation (for lesson 9). Read Job xxvi and xxviii, in the R. V. if possible.

What is the difference between Job xxvi. 6–14 as a description of the universe, and the language of a modern handbook of physiography?

Or,

Learn by heart Ps. xxxvi. 5–9.

Lesson 9

IMAGERY

Its Main Uses.

WE now come to the collective use of imagery, which includes all the literary figures already mentioned. Imagery is language that images or reflects things that are beyond literal description. It is used in the Old Testament for two main purposes:

i. To image the nature of God, i.e. to explain to pagan hearers what God was like;

ii. To give to the suffering Jews a glowing picture of good times to come for Israel.

God imaged in Nature.

i. The first problem was to suggest the power, infinity, and eternity of God by means of such images or reflections as nature could offer, for as nature reflects its creator, the poet naturally takes his imagery from nature itself.

Ps. xxxvi. 5–9 provides a good instance :

v. 5 Thy lovingkindness, O Lord, is *in the heavens* ;
Thy faithfulness reacheth *unto the skies.*

6 Thy righteousness is *like the mountains of God* ;
Thy judgements are *a great deep.*
O Lord, thou preservest man and beast.

7 How precious is thy lovingkindness, O God !
And the children of men take refuge under the shadow of thy wings.

8 They shall be abundantly satisfied with the fatness of thy house ;
And thou shalt make them drink of the *river* of thy pleasures.

9 For with thee is the *fountain* of life :
In thy *light* shall we see light.

Here the poet has selected all the chief features of natural scenery, and made them images of corresponding qualities of God. His love extends to infinity like the *skies*; his righteousness is as great and stable as the *mountains*; his justice is deep as the *sea*; his pleasures are full and flowing as a *river*; human life springs from him like a *fountain*; human light or inspiration is the outcome only of the created *light*.

Power of God in Action.

If the poet wished to describe the power of God in action or operation, he usually composed his picture of God coming to the rescue out of imagery drawn from either (*a*) a storm, or (*b*) the memory of the miraculous crossing of the Red Sea. Of the former take as an instance Ps. xviii. 6–17.

(a) Imagery from a Storm.

v. 6 In my distress I called upon the Lord,
    And cried unto my God :
    He heard my voice out of his temple,
    And my cry before him came into his ears.

7 Then the earth shook and trembled,
    The foundations also of the mountains moved
    And were shaken, because he was wroth.

8 There went up a *smoke* out of his nostrils,
    And *fire* out of his mouth devoured :
    Coals were kindled by it.

9 He bowed the heavens also and came down ;
    And thick *darkness* was under his feet.

10 And he rode upon a cherub, and did fly :
    Yea, he flew swiftly upon *the wings of the wind*.

11 He made *darkness* his hiding place, his pavilion round about him ;
    Darkness of waters, thick clouds of the skies.

12 At the brightness before him his *thick clouds passed*,
    Hailstones and coals of fire.

13 The Lord also *thundered* in the heavens,
    And the Most High uttered his voice ;
    Hailstones and coals of fire.

14 And he sent out his arrows, and scattered them ;
    Yea, *lightnings* manifold, and discomfited them.

15 Then the *channels of waters* appeared,
    And the foundations of the world were laid bare,
    At thy rebuke, O Lord,
    At the *blast* of the breath of thy nostrils.

16 He sent from on high, he took me;
   He drew me out of many waters.
17 He delivered me from my strong enemy,
   And from them that hated me, for they were too mighty for me.

The phenomena of a storm are obvious, but their order is not too clear. An earthquake heralds the approach of God, followed as usual by a fire; then God descends in all the confusion of the storm, bowing[1] or rending the heavens (with his lightning), his feet upon the black clouds, sweeping along with the hurricane (the 'wings of the wind'). The darkness which he has made his 'pavilion' is suddenly broken by the lightning (his 'brightness'), and discharges showers of hailstones. The Most High utters his 'voice' in thunder, and pours out his arrows, the lightnings.

The passage is a majestic one; its impressiveness will be found to depend greatly upon the pagan notion of God wearing human shape, his *nostrils* breathing out lightnings, his *feet* resting on the clouds, &c. This is a mere figure of speech with the Hebrew poet. The Greek gods in Homer drive in chariots and come down to earth with a smell of sulphur, when they scorch the ground. The Greek saw his gods too clearly as a kind of supermen. The Hebrew poet does not try to penetrate the clouds, and his metaphor, while sublime, leaves the mystery as it must be left,

'he maketh the clouds his chariot, and rideth upon the wings of the wind.'[2]

Cowper's hymn of course borrows the same imagery:

> God moves in a mysterious way,
>   His wonders to perform;
> *He plants his footsteps in the sea,*
>   *And rides upon the storm.*

(b) *Imagery from the Passage of the Red Sea.*

The picture of God as the strong deliverer also derives its imagery frequently from the memory of the passage of the

---

[1] Compare Ps. cxliv. 5, Isa. lxiv. 1.   [2] Ps. civ. 3.

Red Sea.   To judge by the constant allusions to it in their
poetry the deliverance from Egypt and the miraculous crossing of the Red Sea fired the Hebrews' imagination more
than any event in their past history.

It is mentioned in plain language in Ps. lxxviii. 13 :

> He clave the sea, and caused them to pass through,
> And he made the waters to stand as an heap.

This suggests the thought or image of the waters retiring
in terror before God, who walks on a highway through the
midst (Ps. lxxvii. 16 f.) :

> The waters saw thee, O God, the waters *saw thee, they were afraid,*
> The depths also *trembled.* . . .
> Thy way was in the sea, and thy paths in the great waters, and
> thy footsteps were not known.

Thus the imaginative poet, treating the waters as alive by
personification.   The language is still more exaggerated by
hyperbole in Ps. cxiv. 1 ff. :

> When Israel went forth out of Egypt. . . .
> *The sea saw it, and fled* ; Jordan was driven back.
> *The mountains skipped like rams, the little hills like young sheep.*

This is continued in an apostrophe, so-called, the sea itself
being addressed,

> What aileth thee, O thou sea, that thou fleest ? . . .
> Tremble, thou earth, at the presence of the Lord.

This image then became a commonplace, and appears in other
forms, other details of the crossing of the Red Sea being
recalled :

> His rod shall be over the sea,
> And he shall lift it up after the manner of Egypt.[1]

(This alludes to Moses's rod, which the poet has transferred
to God's hand.)

> Thou didst tread the sea with thine horses,
> The heap of mighty waters.[2]

[1] Isa. x. 26.   [2] Hab. iii. 15.

Compare also Isa. xliii. 16 with the refrain of Miriam's song in Exod. xv. 4, 5, 10, and the fine picture of God's march before his people in Ps. lxviii. The imagery is the halo which the poets put round the migration of a tribe of nomads.

God as the God of Mercy.

God as the God of mercy is also reflected through suitable imagery. By virtue of his readiness to save, this God of power and might became also the God of mercy and gentleness. The writer of the second part of Isaiah seems to delight in contrasting the terrors and the tenderness of God, his infinite gentleness with his infinite strength:

> 'Behold, the Lord God will come *as a mighty one*, and his arm shall rule for him ... He shall *feed his flock like a shepherd, he shall gather the lambs in his arm, and carry them in his bosom, and shall gently lead those that give suck.*'[1]

Again,

> 'The Lord shall go forth as a mighty man, he shall stir up jealousy like a man of war: ... he shall do mightily against his enemies,'

to which we find this extraordinary corollary

> 'that he may *bring the blind by a way that they know not, and make darkness light before them.*'[2]

'A bruised reed shall he not break' is the image that expresses the gentleness of Jehovah's servant.

The Psalmist too brings God's infinite strength into the closest connexion with his infinite gentleness:

> 'He telleth the number of the stars; he giveth them all their names, Great is our Lord, and mighty in power; His understanding is infinite. The Lord *upholdeth the meek.*'[3]

The most poetical image in this connexion is to be found in Ps. lxxii, remarkable for its conception of God's ideal king, and containing this fine simile (v. 6):

> 'He shall come down *like rain upon the mown grass*, as showers that water the earth.'

[1] Isa. xl. 10 f.   [2] Isa. xlii. 13, 16.

[3] Ps. cxlvii. 4–6. Cf. lxviii. 5, cxlvi. 6–9, Isa. lvii. 15. The Greek respected the stranger and the beggar, and made provision for the orphans in his law, v. Murray, *Rise of the Greek Epic*, p. 108.

Humanity taught by this Imagery.

From these images, and from the attention given to the stranger, the orphan, and the widow, in the Mosaic law, we can see the close connexion between the Hebrews' conception of God and their social ideals. The O.T. steadily insists on this view of God and this duty of man, of which the outcome is that the weak shall not go to the wall. 'Do justice' is coupled with 'love mercy', a combination much softer and kindlier than the cold and stern elevation of justice in Plato's ideal state or in Roman practice. This protection of the helpless because of their helplessness anticipates the notions of modern chivalry. There are parallel ideas in other nations' laws and literature, but no other people gave them such prominence. They are the kernel of the Old Testament revelation. With examples of barbarity all round them the Jewish prophets and poets steadily held up this ideal. The imagery they use is a constant reproof of the harshness they saw practised by their own fellow-countrymen[1] or by the neighbouring peoples. The gods of other nations demanded sacrifices; the Lord Jehovah wanted 'mercy and not sacrifice'.[2] He was imaged in his actions and rulings; he 'heareth the needy and despiseth not the prisoners', he 'healeth the broken in heart and bindeth up their wounds'.[3] It was not surprising that the people who grasped this so clearly and produced such gracious imagery[4] should have been chosen to give birth to Christianity.

Preparation (for lesson 9). Read Isa. xi and xxxiv and xxxv. Show from these chapters and others the prominence of animals in the scheme of these pictures of desolation and restoration.

Or, Learn by heart Isa. xi. 5-9.

[1] For the censure of the prophets directed against sweated labour and cheating of the poor or profiteering, see Amos v. 11, viii. 5, 6, and compare the picture in Job (xxiv. 11).

[2] Hos. vi. 6.   [3] Mic. vi. 8.

[4] Note that the prisoner, the widow, and other weak folk are not always to be taken literally, but often symbolically of helplessness of all kinds, spiritual as well as physical. So Jesus in the Sermon on the Mount takes hunger and thirst in a spiritual sense.

Lesson 10

IMAGERY (continued)

Pictures of Restoration.

ii. THE second purpose for which imagery is chiefly used, especially by the prophets, is to paint the future restoration of the oppressed Jewish nation.

Images are gathered into a picture. One of the most famous of these pictures is Isa. xxxv, a companion picture to Isa. xxxiv, which depicts the desolation that is going to fall on Israel's enemy Edom. The composition of these pictures is interesting. In the first the pride of the land, the great herds of the Edomites, are killed off; then exaggerated or hyperbolical language expresses the ruin and defilement of the countryside, which becomes a desert waste. Its ruined palaces and cities are then peopled with wild and horrible creatures. In the next chapter the process is reversed in reference to Judah :

v. 1 The wilderness [1] and the solitary place shall be glad; and the desert shall rejoice, and blossom as the rose.

2 It shall blossom abundantly, and rejoice even with joy and singing; the glory of Lebanon shall be given unto it : they shall see the glory of the Lord, the excellency of our God.

3 Strengthen ye the weak hands, and confirm the feeble knees.

4 Say to them that are of a fearful heart, Be strong, fear not : behold, your God will come with vengeance, with the recompence of God; he will come and save you.

5 Then the eyes of the blind [2] shall be opened, and the ears of the deaf shall be unstopped.

6 Then shall the lame man leap as an hart, and the tongue of the dumb shall sing : for in the wilderness shall waters break out, and streams in the desert.

7 And the glowing sand [3] shall become a pool, and the thirsty ground springs

[1] The land is first revived and made fit for the exiles' return. All the best things in Palestine spring up again, cedars like Lebanon's, roses like Sharon's.

[2] The severest physical afflictions are cured, (hyperboles to express the joy of the redeemed, as they flock back singing and rejoicing).

[3] The mirage of the desert shall cease to

of water: in the habitation of jackals, where they lay, shall be grass with reeds and rushes.

8 And a high way shall be there, and a way, and it shall be called The way of holiness; the unclean shall not pass over it; but it shall be for those: the wayfaring men, yea fools, shall not err therein.

cheat the traveller. Oases abound. A plain road is made for the exiles' safe convoy, the simplest person cannot miss it.

9 No lion shall be there, nor shall any ravenous beast go up thereon, they shall not be found there; but the redeemed shall walk there:

Wild animals retire.

10 And the ransomed of the Lord shall return, and come with singing unto Zion; and everlasting joy shall be upon their heads: They shall obtain gladness and joy, and sorrow and sighing shall flee away.

The 'ransomed' enter Zion in triumph.

The above is not a picture merely of the restoration of Judaea. It symbolizes also the spiritual restoration of the chosen people. But it will be noticed that the imagery used is of such a general kind that a passage, which was intended primarily for the Jew, became applicable to all people for all time. Though the scene is oriental everybody can understand the terms 'blind', 'dumb', and 'lame' in a figurative sense.

At the same time much of the imagery is literally applicable to the work of Jesus in his ministry, when 'the lame walked, the dumb spake, the blind received their sight'.[1] Even Jesus did these cures, however, as signs of what he could do for the spirit.

Other pictures of restoration, almost equally beautiful, borrow their imagery from precious stones, from light arising out of darkness, or from human relationships.

Precious stones.

'O thou afflicted, tossed with tempest, and not comforted,
Behold, I will set thy stones in fair colours, and lay thy foundations with sapphires.

[1] Compare Acts iii. 8, the lame man 'leaping up, stood and began to walk, and entered . . . into the temple, walking, and leaping, and praising God'.

And I will make thy pinnacles of rubies, and thy gates of carbuncles, and all thy border of pleasant stones.

And all thy children shall be taught of the Lord; and great shall be the peace of thy children.' Isa. liv. 11–14.

Compare with this the imagery of the New Jerusalem in Rev. xxi. 18–21, which was evidently inspired by this passage.

Light.

'Arise, shine; for thy light is come, and the glory of the Lord is risen upon thee.

For, behold, darkness shall cover the earth, and gross darkness the peoples:

but the Lord shall arise upon thee, and his glory shall be seen upon thee.

And nations shall come to thy light, and kings to the brightness of thy rising.

(The passage proceeds to promise an influx of wealth into Judaea, and gives a picture of the rich convoys entering the land from all countries. It then goes on with the original imagery.)

The sun shall be no more thy light by day; neither for brightness shall the moon give light unto thee; but the Lord shall be unto thee an everlasting light, and thy God thy glory.

Thy sun shall no more go down, neither shall thy moon withdraw itself: for the Lord shall be thine everlasting light, and the days of thy mourning shall be ended.' Isa. lx. 1–3, 19 f.

This beautiful imagery, derived entirely from the single idea of 'light', should again be compared with the imagery of the New Jerusalem in Revelation (xxi. 11 and 23).

Human relationships.

'Thou shalt no more be termed Forsaken; neither shall thy land any more be termed Desolate:

But thou shalt be termed Hephzi-bah (i.e. my delight is in her), and thy land Beulah (i.e. married):

For the Lord delighteth in thee, and thy land shall be married.

For as a young man marrieth a virgin, so shall thy sons marry thee:

and as the bridegroom rejoiceth over the bride, so shall thy God rejoice over thee.' Isa. lxii. 4 f.

Compare also the frequent descriptions of Judah as a widow.

Equally famous is the picture of the peace brought by the
Messiah, in which the imagery is derived from animal life,
the prophet *imagining* the brute beasts at peace with one
another. The fiercest animals are grouped together, cease
preying upon one another, and suffer a child to lead them.

> 'And the wolf shall dwell with the lamb, and the leopard shall
> lie down with the kid ; and the calf and the young lion and the
> fatling together ; and a little child shall lead them.
> And the cow and the bear shall feed ; their young ones shall
> lie down together : and the lion shall eat straw like the ox.
> And the sucking child shall play on the hole of the asp, and
> the weaned child shall put his hand on the basilisk's den.
> They shall not hurt nor destroy in all my holy mountain : for
> the earth shall be full of the knowledge of the Lord, as the
> waters cover the sea. Isa. xi. 6–9.

Meaning of the Imagery.

In the above pictures of jewels or animals note, so to
speak, the fullness of the canvas, especially in the last illustration. It is perhaps in these prophecies of the future
restoration of their race that the literary genius of the
Hebrews shows itself at its greatest. The prophet is stirred
by the misfortunes of his countrymen. But he feels there
must be compensation to come, and in view of Jehovah's
promise of old it is bound to be in full measure, and rich
beyond belief. It will be something far greater than restoration of money or goods. The reward will bring consolation
of spirit. But as a spiritual reward may not appeal to the
uninstructed sense of his audience he falls back upon images
of a more satisfying nature, and uses them in rich variety.
The rhythm and choice of diction of the English translation
are of course remarkable, and convey something of the dignity
and balance of the original language.

Effect upon the Style.

A clear example of the way in which imagery elevates the
style will be found in Isa. lviii, where the prophet is reminding
the Jews of their simple duties, and of the rewards that will
follow their performance. The duties are named in plain

language but the reward in poetical images. Compare vv. 6, 7, ' deal thy bread to the hungry . . . . ' with v. 8, ' *Then shall thy light break forth as the morning,* and thy healing shall spring forth speedily: and thy righteousness *shall go before thee*; the glory of the Lord *shall be thy rearward* . . . . And thou shalt be *like a watered garden, and like a spring of water* . . . .' Compare also v. 13, ' if thou shalt . . . . honour the sabbath,' with v. 14, ' *I will make thee to ride upon the high places of the earth.*'

Exercises. 1. Isa. xlix and Zech. viii both foretell the future fame of Jerusalem, even amongst the Gentiles. Make a list of the imagery and literary figures used in each passage; note any that correspond; show which style is the more poetical.

2. Read Isa. lix. 4-10, 16-18. Show how the images develop in a kind of progression, a word in one verse suggesting the metaphor in the next.

Preparation (for lesson 11). Read Ps. civ, cxlvii, and Job xxxviii-xl.

VIII

Lesson 11

IMAGERY *and the* HEBREW VIEW *of* NATURE

IT is always interesting to see how poets of a particular nationality feel towards nature. The similes and metaphors which they use are a guide. The greater part of the imagery of the O.T. is drawn from nature.

We shall not expect to find in the O.T. those feelings towards the beauty of natural objects which Wordsworth felt. With Wordsworth it was a 'cult' to look for beauty in nature and find it and talk about it. Take for instance the simile about the maiden :

> A violet by a mossy stone
>   Half hidden from the eye,
> Fair as a star, when only one
>   Is shining in the sky.[1]

A Hebrew might have used the violet by way of comparison, as he used the lily and the rose of Sharon, but he would not have stopped to analyse the special beauty of a violet 'half hidden by a mossy stone'. The lily was beautiful and that was enough. Three British poets[2] have given us studies of skylarks. The only thing a Hebrew poet would have found time to notice in a skylark is its special qualifications for praising its Maker. If there were any song-birds in Palestine they are not mentioned.[3] Shelley again compares something with

> 'mountain springs under the morning sun.'

---

[1] 'Lucy Gray.'   [2] Shelley, Hogg, Wordsworth.
[3] If we except the 'mourning' of doves.

A Hebrew poet does indeed notice the brightness of the morning sun free from clouds,[1] but would not, one feels, have noticed the particular effect of it upon water.

The Hebrew saw in nature the work of a strong hand rather than the beauty and variety that the modern eye has been trained to see. Allowance must also be made for the difference of scenery. But to the Hebrew each natural object seems to have suggested a single quality or characteristic, and that quality was rarely beauty. For instance, to him the chief feature of a flower was its rapid fading, and it appears as an image only of the shortness of human life. Contrast the following verdict:

> A lily of a day
> Is fairer far, in May,
> Although it fall and die that night,
> It was the plant and flower of light.   (Ben Jonson.)

The lily here does not simply point a moral about 'change and decay', it is the 'thing of beauty (that) is a joy for ever'.

Natural objects in the Old Testament are images or reflections of God, and are noticed for some single prominent feature:

(a) *Mountains* suggested strength and durability:

> God's 'righteousness is like the strong mountains'. Ps.xxxvi. 6.
> 'As the mountains are round about Jerusalem, so the Lord is round about his people.' Ps. cxxv. 2.
> 'Before the mountains were brought forth ..., from everlasting to everlasting thou art God.'
> Ps. xc. 2, cf. Job xv. 7, Deut. xxxiii. 15.
> 'By his strength setteth fast the mountains.' Ps. lxv. 6.

The beautiful outlines, rolling slopes, and light effects of the mountains are not noticed, only their strength and durability.

(b) *Rivers*, such as the Nile, suggest strength in motion. The following metaphor shows the terrible advance of the Assyrians:

> 'The Lord bringeth up upon them the waters of the River, strong and many, and he shall come up over all his channels, and go over all his banks: and he shall sweep onward into Judah ... he shall reach even to the neck.' Isa. viii. 7, 8.

[1] 2 Sam. xxiii. 4.

The streams in Palestine, when they do not stand merely for the precious water supply 'in a thirsty land', either suggest force when in flood, or instability when dried up, because in Palestine a rushing torrent may soon become a dry channel. They did not, like Tennyson's brook, go on for ever. The charm of a stream, its rippling transparency, or the murmur that invites sleep, are not mentioned.[1]

(c) The *Sea* again suggested to the Hebrew only immense strength; it was not a thing of beauty, of 'infinite variety'. It was full of wonders, but of a terrible kind, the home of strange monsters, 'things creeping innumerable',[2] making a terrible noise, like the roar of approaching enemies,[3] horrible as the pit or grave to those who like Jonah remembered its dank weeds and depths,[4] an emblem to Isaiah of the restless wicked 'casting up mire and dirt'.[5]

(d) *Animals* also are noticed for their strength or wonderful motion as things of terror rather than of beauty. It is the strong and wild animals that are mentioned most frequently, the lion, the wild ass, the unicorn, the wild ox ('canst thou bind him?'), behemoth ('his limbs are like bands of iron'), leviathan ('in his neck abideth strength, and terror danceth before him'). Even the horse is mentioned only for its strength, and the fine description of one in Job is of the war-horse ('the glory of his snorting is terrible').[6]

So it is with *birds*. The eagle is quoted numberless times for its strength of flight or its terror as a bird of prey, and its habits and those of doves have been keenly noted, but the song and plumage of birds are rarely noticed.[7]

So it is with *children*. Children were interesting if there were plenty of them, a 'quiverful', so that the father might 'hold up his head in the gate',[8] but no similes are derived

---

[1] The nearest approach to a suggestion of beauty in rivers is in Isa. lxvi. 12, 'I will extend peace to her like a river.' Cf. Isa. xlviii. 18.

[2] Ps. civ. 25.   [3] Isa. v. 30.   [4] Jonah ii. 5.   [5] Isa. lvii. 20.

[6] Job xxxix–xli. Cf. Burke, *On the Sublime and Beautiful*, Pt. II, 5.

[7] Ps. lxviii. 13, Isa. lix. 11, Nahum ii. 7, Job xxxix. 13. (See also *note* on page 77).   [8] Ps. cxxvii. 5.

from observing the habits and innocence of childhood, though Zechariah pictures them playing in the streets of the restored Zion.[1]

It will be found then that

1. one prominent feature is selected for comparison from all natural objects, e. g. the eagle's swiftness, the mountain's strength, the ant's wisdom, the stream's instability;
2. it is the stern side of nature that comes under observation as a rule. This would largely be due to the nature of the scenery in Palestine;
3. nature is merely a mirror of God's strength, majesty, and power.

Everything in nature is a servant of the Creator, and waits upon him. The wonderful nature psalms are not praises of nature but of God through nature. That is why the poets dwell on those animals which to man are apparently useless, the key to their existence being that God made them, to receive honour from the meanest of them. 'The jackals and the ostriches shall honour me, because I give waters in the wilderness'.[2] It is never suggested that wild animals were made for the chase, on the contrary, they are the peculiar care of Providence. The lion 'gets his meat from God',[3] the conies or rabbits have rocks provided for them as a refuge.[4] Note especially that the wicked Nineveh is spared not only for the thousands of ignorant people in it, but for its 'much cattle'.[5] The ocean, terrible and vast as it is, is God's servant, and 'lifts up its hands' to him. 'Above the voice of many waters, the mighty breakers of the sea, the Lord on high is mighty.'[6]

All the phenomena of nature are viewed in a similar light. The snow that 'is given like wool', the hoar frost 'scattered like ashes', the grass that 'is made to grow upon the mountains' are only additional means of gauging the divine power. The grass for instance is a wonderful provision for the cattle,

---

[1] Zech. viii. 5.   [2] Isa. xliii. 20.   [3] Ps. civ. 21.
[4] Ibid., v. 18.   [5] Jonah iv. 11.   [6] Ps. xciii. 4.

and not made to beautify the landscape. The Hebrew did not rejoice in nature for its *beauty*. He rejoiced in *God* for nature's wonderful resources and strength.

Note. It is chiefly in the Song of Solomon, a work of late composition, that we get references to the grace and beauty of animals, like the fawn, or to the soft eyes of doves. The feeling for beauty in nature is supposed to come late in a people's artistic development. Proverbs (xxx. 19, 29) mentions the motion of various animals, and Isaiah (lx. 8) compares ships with doves returning to their cotes. These instances are not sufficient to affect the main conclusions derived above.

Preparation (for lesson 12). Read Judges v and Hab. iii.

From the song of Deborah in Judges v reconstruct, as far as possible, the battle of Kishon and the circumstances preceding it.

Lesson 12

OTHER LITERARY DEVICES

In addition to the imagery already illustrated, similes, metaphors, allegory, hyperboles, and personifications, the Hebrew writers use the following oratorical devices to give energy and animation to their style :

(1) The *repetition of a word*, a favourite device of the writer of the second part of Isaiah, rousing like a trumpet call :

'Awake, awake, put on strength, O arm of the Lord.' Isa. li. 9.
'Go through, go through the gates.' Isa. lxii. 10.
'Comfort ye, comfort ye, my people, saith your God.' Isa. xl. 1.

(2) The *exclamations* are no less stirring, suddenly interrupting the discourse :

'How beautiful upon the mountains are the feet of him that bringeth good tidings !' Isa. lii. 7.
'How is the faithful city become an harlot !' Isa. i. 21.
'How are the mighty fallen, and the weapons of war perished !'
2 Sam. i. 27.

(3) The *sudden question* :

(*a*) clinching an argument :

'This is the purpose that is purposed on the whole earth :
And this is the hand that is stretched out upon all the nations.
For the Lord of Hosts hath purposed, *and who shall disannul it*?
And his hand is stretched out, *and who shall turn it back*?'
Isa. xiv. 26.
'The lion hath roared, *who will not fear*?
The Lord God hath spoken, *who can but prophesy*?' Amos iii. 8.

(*b*) conveying a challenge :

'Who hath believed our report? And to whom hath the arm of the Lord been revealed?' Isa. liii. 1.
'Hast thou not known? Hast thou not heard? The everlasting God fainteth not, neither is weary.' Isa. xl. 28.

(*c*) relieving the monotony of a long recital :

'Who are these that fly as a cloud, and as the doves to their windows ?' Isa. lx. 8.

(4) The figure called *apostrophe*, or 'turning away' suddenly from the discourse to address some one in the second person ; the finest instance of this is the close of Deborah's song in Judges v. The singer has just created a picture of Sisera's court wondering at his late arrival, the mother of Sisera looking through the lattice window, the ladies speculating upon their share of the spoils. Then the singer suddenly drops the curtain on the picture and puts away her personal vindictive-ness, and remembers the heathen are Jehovah's enemies rather than her own.

> Through the window she looked forth,
> The mother of Sisera cried through the lattice,
> 'Why is his chariot so long in coming?
> Why tarry the wheels of his chariots ? '
> Her wise ladies answered her,
> Yea, she returned answer to herself,
> 'Have they not found, have they not divided the spoil ?
> A damsel, two damsels to every man ;
> To Sisera a spoil of divers colours,
> A spoil of divers colours of embroidery,
> Of divers colours of embroidery on both sides, on the necks of the spoil ? '
> *So let all thine enemies perish, O Lord :*
> *But let them that love him be as the sun when he goeth forth in his might.*

We may also compare the song in Deut. xxxii, which is mostly in the third person, but where the singer in his emotion turns three times to address the people directly, vv. 6, 15, 18.

Summary of Imagery and Literary Devices.

The lyric in Hab. iii is one of the finest examples of Hebrew poetry. It describes God's triumphant march to battle to justify his elect, in all its majesty and terror, and it contains in a small compass perhaps more of the literary devices above described than any other passage. It does more. It contains the kernel of the teaching of the Old Testament. In v. 16 the poet stands cowering while God punishes the wicked. Their ruin is his ruin too, the land is desolate and he with it. His trees are blasted, his garden waste, his sheep and oxen driven off. But his jealousy for righteousness is satisfied, the wicked oppressor has not gone unpunished; his own goods are gone, but his faith is saved in Jehovah and the right. He has rest, even joy, in the day of trouble. ' The just lives by his faith ' (ii. 4). This chapter illustrates very well the attitude which Matthew Arnold describes in the famous passage of ' Obermann (Once More) ' :

> The brooding East with awe beheld
>   Her impious younger world ;
> The Roman tempest swelled and swelled,
>   And on her head was hurled.
>
> The East bow'd low before the blast,
>   In patient deep disdain.
> She let the legions thunder past,
>   Then plunged in thought again.
>
> So well she mused, a morning broke
>   Across her spirit grey.
> A conquering new-born joy awoke
>   And filled her life with day.
>
> ' Poor world ', she cried, ' so deep accurst !
>   That runn'st from pole to pole
> To seek a draught to slake thy thirst !—
>   Go, seek it in thy soul.'

If we substitute Babylon for the Roman, the above would represent very well the point of view of Habakkuk when he has seen the invasion of the Chaldaeans, and the wickedness it was meant to punish.

Note. The ode below is printed from the revised version, but the meaning of several verses is variously given by scholars. In the first chapter the prophet seems to attack the wickedness of his own countrymen, and then suddenly to denounce the Chaldaeans who have been appointed by God to avenge it. But the difficulties of interpretation will not affect the present purpose, which is to examine the imagery and literary aspect of it.

*Hab. iii, a Hebrew lyric, describing God's march to rescue
his people, and to punish the wicked*

v. 2 O Lord, I have heard the report of thee,
     and am afraid :
          O Lord, revive thy work in the midst
          of the years,
          In the midst of the years make it known ;
          In wrath remember mercy.

   3 God came from Teman,
          And the Holy One from Mount Paran.
          His glory covered the heavens,
          And the earth was full of his praise.
   4 And his brightness was as the light,
          He had rays coming forth from his hand :
          And there was the hiding of his power.
   5 Before him went the pestilence,
          And fiery bolts went forth at his feet.
   6 He stood, and measured the earth ;
          He beheld, and drove asunder the
          nations :
          And the eternal mountains were scat-
          tered,
          The everlasting hills did bow ;
          His goings were as of old.

   7 I saw the tents of Cushan in affliction :
          The curtains of the land of Midian did
          tremble.
   8 Was the Lord displeased against the
          rivers ?
          Was thine anger against the rivers,
          Or thy wrath against the sea,
          That thou didst ride upon thine horses,
          Upon thy chariots of salvation ?

   9 Thy bow was made quite bare ;
          The oaths to the tribes were a sure
          word.
          Thou didst cleave the earth with rivers.
  10 The mountains saw thee, and were
          afraid ;
          The tempest of waters passed by :
          The deep uttered his voice,
          And lifted up his hands on high.
  11 The sun and moon stood still in their
          habitation ;

The imagery is like that of Ps. xviii (see p. 64). Light and lightnings mark God's appearance. Pestilence goes before, an earthquake shakes the nations and mountains, and all nature looks on in terror, while God advances like a great army, with bow and arrows, spear, char-iots, and horses.

N.B. i. the similes, vv. 4, 14, 19.

ii. metaphor, v. 12 (thresh).

iii. personification, v. 10.

iv. hyperbole, v. 6, 'mountains scatter-ed,' 'hills bowing,' v. 11, 'sun standing still.'

v. sudden question expressing scorn, v. 8.

vi. Apostrophe, v. 8, 'Was thine anger against the rivers ?'

N.B. also the local allusion in v. 7, to give a touch of reality

At the light of thine arrows as they went,
At the shining of thy glittering spear.
12 Thou didst march through the land in
indignation,
Thou didst thresh the nations in anger.
13 Thou wentest forth for the salvation of
thy people,
For the salvation of thine anointed ;

.   .   .   .

14 Thou didst pierce with his own staves
the head of his warriors :
They came as a whirlwind to scatter me :
Their rejoicing was as to devour the
poor secretly.
15 Thou didst tread the sea with thine
horses,
The heap of mighty waters.

16 I heard and my belly trembled,
My lips quivered at the voice ;
Rottenness entered into my bones, and
I trembled in my place :
That I should rest in the day of trouble,
When it cometh up against the people
which invadeth him in troops.
17 For though the fig tree shall not blossom,
Neither shall fruit be in the vines ;
The labour of the olive shall fail,
And the fields shall yield no meat ;
The flock shall be cut off from the fold,
And there shall be no herd in the stalls ;
18 Yet I will rejoice in the Lord,
I will joy in the God of my salvation.
19 Jehovah, the Lord, is my strength,
And he maketh my feet like hinds' feet,
And will make me to walk upon mine
high places.

in the midst of the imagery and figures, and the anthropomorphism, vv. 4, 5, 8, &c. (see p. 64, note on Psalm xviii).

The vine, the fig, and the olive associated as usual in the Old Testament.

Exercises.   (See example on next page.)

1. Write a Hebraic ode on one of the following subjects, using the imagery and figures already analysed :
   (*a*) The deliverance of France by Joan of Arc, put into the mouth of a French poet.
   (*b*) The Plague of London, regarded as a divine judgement, put into the mouth of a persecuted Puritan.

   Or,

 2. Compose a Hebraic prophecy of the slave emancipation in America, as foretold by some Virginian negro in the early part of the nineteenth century.

Preparation (for lesson 13). Read Isa. liii, 'the suffering servant'. Make a list of the verbs and nouns that express the *suffering* of the Man of Sorrows.

   Or,

   Learn by heart Isa. xl. 28–31.

 The following is suggested as the kind of ode which a Hebrew prophet might have composed upon the defeat of the Spanish Armada. It is modelled on Judges v and Habakkuk iii.

Defeat of the Spanish Armada.

Hear, O ye kings,
Give ear, all ye princes of the earth;
I will sing unto the Lord,
I will sing praises unto the God of Albion.

Prelude.

O Lord, when thou wentest forth from Devon,
When thou didst ride upon the waters,
The tempest went before thee,
The sea was full of thy praise.
The promontories saw thy lightnings and were troubled,
The deep uttered his voice and lifted up his hands on high.
Thine enemies sank in the overflowing of the waves.

Great stress will of course be laid upon the storm that reduced the Spanish fleet.

The proud are robbed, the oppressor is brought low;
Their ships are vanished from the face of the waters.
They gathered their ships in the south;
They devised a yoke of iron for the necks of thy people, O Lord.
Then did the beacons shine forth from the Cornish hills;
The seamen of Wessex watched in their rivers.
Was the heart of thine Anointed afraid?
Or did confusion reign in the Queen's counsels?

Sudden question (see p. 78) refering to Queen Elizabeth.

My heart is toward the mariners of Devon,
Because they came to the help of the Lord,
To the help of the Lord against the mighty.
They jeoparded their lives unto the death,
In the channels of waters.   Praise ye the Lord.

The winds blew from heaven,
The winds fought against Philip ;
His galleons are broken,
At thy rebuke, O Lord, they are scattered upon   The Orkneys, &c.
    the headlands.
Fear shall come upon Arragon,
Sorrow shall take hold of the princes of Castile.
They built high the decks,
They sailed to seize the prey, line upon line ;
Their boasting was to devour the folk by fire and   The Inquisition is
    tortures.   referred to.

Ascribe ye strength unto God ;   Finale.
His excellence is over Albion,
And his strength is in the heavens.
We will rejoice in the Lord ;
We will rejoice in the God of our salvation.
The Lord, he it is that giveth power unto his
    Anointed.
Strengthen, O Lord, that which thou hast
    wrought in us.
Blessed be God.

Lesson 13

DICTION

'In Hebrew as in Arabic the best writing is an unaffected transcription of the best speaking. . . . The literary merit of the book of Genesis or the history of Elijah is that they read as if they were told by word of mouth.'— Robertson Smith, *Prophets of Israel*, p. 146.

VIGOUR and simplicity are the chief qualities of such a style. The simplicity of Amos was mistaken by earlier commentators for rusticity. On the contrary, 'it is a token of complete mastery over a language which is unsurpassed as a vehicle of impassioned speech'.—*Ibid.*

(*a*) The **simplicity and restraint** of the style have already been noted [1] in the chapter on narrative. It will perhaps have been noticed that the style is never more simple and restrained than when the ways of God are being described, as, for instance, in the creation, '*the spirit of God moved upon* the face of the waters'.[2] Or again, 'God said, Let there be light, and there was light'. In the crossing of the Red Sea, 'it came to pass in the morning watch, that the Lord *looked forth* upon the host of the Egyptians through the pillar of fire and of cloud, and *discomfited* the host of the Egyptians'.[3] One look of God overwhelms hosts, which may have inspired Byron's fine lines on the destruction of Sennacherib's forces,

> And the hosts of the heathen unsmote by the sword,
> Had melted like snow *in the glance of the Lord.*

(*b*) The **compactness and vigour** of the diction are less easy to appreciate in a translation. A fair impression may be gained by following the Authorized Version, and omitting

---

[1] See Chapter X on p. 30.   [2] Gen. i. 2, 3.   [3] Exod. xiv. 24.

words in italics, when it will be noticed that certain features
of the Hebrew verb-forms, and the omission of the verb
'to be' and of many of the pronouns and prepositions, make
the original even more concise than the translation. For
example,

> Where shall wisdom be found . . .?
> The depth saith, Not in me . . .[1]

Metaphor also helps to make the diction vigorous and
concise. E. g. 'If thou doest not well, sin *coucheth* at the
door'.[2] The Authorized Version had 'lieth', but the word
refers to the attitude of a wild beast waiting to spring. In
Jonah (i. 13), where the Revised Version says 'the men rowed
hard to get them back to land', the Hebrew has 'they *dug the
sea*'. Judah, in his appeal to Joseph, speaks of Jacob's life
as bound up with that of Benjamin, for which the Hebrew
has, 'his soul is *knit* with the lad's soul',[3] and in the Song of
Moses, 'Jeshurun *waxed fat and kicked*' expresses the laziness
and grossness of Israel.[4] In the verse, 'weeping may *tarry*
for the night, but joy cometh in the morning', 'tarry' represents in the Hebrew '*cometh in to lodge*', i. e. grief only stays
for a single night's lodging.[5] These instances of incorporated
metaphor could be multiplied by scholars.

A good instance[6] of compactness of diction is furnished by
Job iii. 3 ff.:

> Let the day perish wherein I was born,
> And the night *which said*, There is a man child conceived.

This is the fierce curse of a man overwhelmed with tragedy.
Jeremiah waters it down into a pitiful complaint, by lengthen-
ing the lines and drawing them out into two couplets:

> Cursed be the day wherein I was born:
> Let not the day wherein my mother bare me be blessed.
> Cursed be the man who brought tidings to my father,
> Saying, A man child is born unto thee; making him very
>   glad.   Jer. xx. 14 f.

[1] Job xxviii. 12-14.   [2] Gen. iv. 7.   [3] Gen. xliv. 30.
[4] Deut. xxxii. 15.   [5] Ps. xxx. 5.
[6] This instance is taken from Lowth's *Lectures on Hebrew Poetry*, vol. i,
p. 317, a book of the eighteenth century, the first perhaps to call attention
to the literary merits of the Old Testament.

The difference between the vigorous, compressed couplet of Job and the drawn-out version of Jeremiah has been expressed as follows: 'the first sounds the note of tragedy, the second that of elegy.'

(c) *The concentration of the diction* upon a single idea, to impress that idea more firmly on the mind, may be illustrated by the famous passage of the 'Man of Sorrows' or 'the righteous servant' in Isa. liii.

In English and Latin literature this result is achieved by the concentration of noun, verb, and epithet in the same sentence upon one idea, as in the following examples:

> With music *lulled* his *indolent repose*.
> > Wordsworth, *Excur.* i. 720.
> > *Sollicitam* timor *anxius angit*. Vergil, *Aen.* ix. 89.
> (*Anxious* fear *wrings* my *troubled* heart.)
> *Tostamque fervens* Iulius *coquit* messem. Martial, x. 62, 7.
> (The *hot* Julian star *bakes* the *scorched* harvest.)

In these examples the epithets at least are not wholly necessary to the meaning, but they help to drive it home, or, so to say, to make atmosphere. The Old Testament writers use epithets more rarely, but they do collect words of similar meaning to create an atmosphere round a central idea. They play skilfully upon words of similar import, with a certain amount of repetition and delicate variations. It is difficult otherwise to account for the effectiveness of the following sentences describing trustfulness from Isa. xxvi. 3, 4:

> 'A *stedfast* mind thou *keepest* in *peace, peace*, because it *trusteth* in thee. *Trust* ye in the Lord for ever, for in the Lord Jehovah is an everlasting rock.'

The method is shown more clearly in the passage of 'the righteous servant' referred to above. This passage may be briefly summarized as follows:

v. 2 God's suffering servant (whose innocent suffering is to redeem his people) is without comeliness or beauty,

3 a man of grief, whom we despised;

4-7 yet his grief was for us, and he bore it without complaint.

8 Who however at the time considered the purpose of it?

9 Though innocent he was classed with the guilty.

10, 11 It was God, however, who was making him a sin-offering, and the sacrifice will bear fruit,

12 and he will share the victory of the strong.

The doctrine of this is striking and unique: 'the second Isaiah discovered the secret of the redemptive power of innocent suffering'.[1] But the literary beauty which now concerns us does not this time spring from the imagery, though the passage is relieved by the simile of the dumb sheep in v. 7. It is due, as was said above, to the skilful play upon words of similar meaning, expressing suffering, delicately varied and sometimes repeated.[2] There are nine different verbs, three of them repeated, and seven different nouns, one of them repeated, to express the treatment meted out to the man of sorrows, besides phrases of similar effect.[3] These culminate in 'the grave', v. 9, and in the fine expression of v. 12, a suitable climax, 'he poured out his soul unto death'. There is a similar play upon sin, iniquities, and transgression, and the English translators, by reserving the longer words for the cadences, preserved the sonority of the rhythm. The passage is thus a kind of mournful but majestic requiem, with a burst of more joyous music at the close,

> I will divide him a portion with the great,
> And he shall divide the spoil with the strong,

sinking again on the last chord into the strains which composed the main theme,

> 'and he bare the sin of many, and made intercession for the transgressors.'

A similar method is used in Isaiah xl. 28-31, where the writer again plays upon one set of words, not only without monotony, but with a kind of progression up to a climax. Those who learn these passages off by heart will not easily forget the haunting rhythm of the diction.

---

[1] *Outline of Literature*, Drinkwater, p. 57.

[2] Notice especially v. 5. There are of course many fine phrases of other kinds besides, which contribute to the beauty of the whole.

[3] In the text the nouns and verbs are differently indicated. The Hebrew has 'sicknesses' for 'grief' in v. 4, and 'made him sick' for 'put him to grief' in v. 10.

Isaiah liii

(The passage really begins at lii. 13, 'Behold, my servant shall deal wisely, ... his visage was so marred ...)

1 Who hath believed our report? and to whom hath the arm of the Lord been revealed?

2 For he grew up before him as a tender plant, and as a root out of a dry ground: he hath no form nor comeliness; and when we see him, there is no beauty that we should desire him.

3 He was *despised* and *rejected* of men; a man of SORROWS, and acquainted with GRIEF: and as one from whom men hide their face he was *despised* and we esteemed him not.

4 Surely he hath borne our GRIEFS, and carried our SORROWS: yet we did esteem him *stricken, smitten* of God, and *afflicted.*

5 But he was *wounded* for our **transgressions,** he was *bruised* for our **iniquities:** the CHASTISEMENT of our peace was upon him; and with his STRIPES we are healed.

6 All we like sheep have gone astray; we have turned every one to his own way; and the Lord hath laid on him the **iniquity** of us all.

7 He was *oppressed,* yet he humbled himself and opened not his mouth; as a lamb that is led to the slaughter, and as a sheep that before her shearers is dumb; yea, he opened not his mouth.

8 By OPPRESSION and judgement he was taken away; and as for his generation, who among them considered that he was cut off out of the land of the living? for the **transgression** of my people was he *stricken.*

9 And they made his grave with the wicked, and with the rich in his death; although he had done no violence, neither was any deceit in his mouth.

10 Yet it pleased the Lord to *bruise* him; he hath *put him to grief:* when thou shalt make his soul an offering for **sin,** he shall see his seed, he shall prolong his days, and the pleasure of the Lord shall prosper in his hand.

11 He shall see of the TRAVAIL of his soul, and shall be satisfied: by his knowledge shall my righteous servant justify many: and he shall bear their **iniquities.**

12 Therefore will I divide him a portion with the great, and he shall divide the spoil with the strong, because he poured out his soul unto death, and was numbered with the **transgressors:** yet he bare the **sin** of many, and made intercession for the **transgressors.**

Isaiah xl. 27–31

Note here the simile strengthening the climax in the last verse, just as that of the lamb supplies a little colour to the former passage.

27 Why sayest thou, O Jacob, and speakest, O Israel, 'My way is hid from the Lord, and my judgement is passed away from my God?'

28 Hast thou not known? hast thou not heard? the everlasting God, the Lord, the Creator of the ends of the earth, *fainteth* not, neither *is weary*; there is no searching of his understanding.

29 He giveth power to the *faint*, and to him that hath no **might**, he increaseth **strength**.

30 Even the youths shall *faint* and *be weary*, and the young men shall utterly fall:

31 But they that wait upon the Lord shall renew their **strength**; they shall mount up with wings as eagles; they shall run, and not *be weary*; they shall walk, and not *faint*.

Preparation (for lesson 14). i. Divide Psalm cvii into stanzas. Why should Psalms xlii and xliii be arranged as one Psalm?

ii. In Psalm cxxi show in which verses the second part of the verse (1) merely echoes the first part, (2) completes the sense of it; and from Proverbs x show what is the third main function of the second part of the verse in Hebrew poetry.

Lesson 14

PARALLELISM

In poetry the ear demands something more than a regular rhythm. This demand may be satisfied by rhyme, as in our English lyrics and elegiac poetry, or by cadences at the end of each line, as in Greek and Roman elegy. In Hebrew poetry the demand is satisfied by balance of thought in addition to balance of rhythm.[1]

Couplets are the commonest form, but there are also triplets and quatrains. Compare Psalm i:

> Blessed is the man that *walketh* not in the counsel of the wicked,
> Nor *standeth* in the way of sinners,
> Nor *sitteth* in the seat of the scornful,'

and for the quatrain compare Psalm cxxvii:

> Except the Lord build the house,
> They labour in vain that build it:
> Except the Lord keep the city,
> The watchman waketh but in vain.

'The best and most perfect specimens of Hebrew poetry are, as a rule, those in which the parallelism is most complete.' Even the prophets, whose diction is usually an elevated prose, fall consciously or unconsciously into the parallel arrangement when they wish to emphasize or enforce their thought.[2] The rarity of it in Hosea is attributed to

[1] R. G. Moulton, *Literary Study of the Bible*, distinguishes between this parallelism and a 'higher' parallelism of structure, applying to the balance of whole odes.

[2] Driver, *Lit. of Old Testament*, quotes Isa. i. 2, 3, 10, &c., xiii. 10-13, Amos vi. 1-7.

the overmastering emotion and grief, which break up his message into so many sighs and cries of anguish.

The second part of the verse either (i) echoes the idea contained in the first part,

> The Lord upholdeth all that fall,
> And raiseth up all those that be bowed down. **Ps. cxlv.** 14.

or (ii) it forms a contrast with it,

> A soft answer turneth away wrath,
> But a grievous word stirreth up anger. **Prov. xv.** 1.

In the latter case, the more striking the words on which the contrast hinges, the more effective, of course, is the parallelism. The beauty of David's lament over Saul and Jonathan will at once occur to the mind:

> Saul and Jonathan were lovely and pleasant in their *lives*,
> And in their *death* they were not divided.
> They were swifter than *eagles*,
> They were stronger than *lions*. **2 Sam. i.** 23.

(iii) The second line may also complete the first by providing the reason or consequence:

> Save me, O God,
> For the waters are come in unto my soul. **Ps. lxix.** 1.

> Why hast thou broken down her fences,
> So that all they which pass by the way do pluck her?
> **Ps. lxxx.** 12.

or, again, it may add a comparison:

> Thy love to me was wonderful,
> Passing the love of women. **2 Sam. i.** 26.

A simile may be divided between the two lines:

> As arrows in the hand of a mighty man,
> So are the children of youth.

The general effect of the parallelism in a passage of any length appears at its best in the following example from Isaiah, where the second part of the verse is a gentle echo of the first:

> For Zion's sake will I not hold my peace,
> And for Jerusalem's sake I will not rest,

> Until her righteousness go forth as brightness,
> And her salvation as a lamp that burneth.
>
> And the nations shall see thy righteousness,
> And all kings thy glory.
>
> And thou shalt be called by a new name,
> Which the mouth of the Lord shall name.
>
> Thou shalt also be a crown of beauty in the hand of the Lord,
> And a royal diadem in the hand of thy God.
>
> Thou shalt no more be termed Forsaken,
> Neither shall thy land any more be termed Desolate.
>
> But thou shalt be called Hephzi-bah,
> And thy land Beulah;
>
> For the Lord delighteth in thee,
> And thy land shall be married.
>
> For as a young man marrieth a virgin,
> So shall thy sons marry thee.
>
> And as the bridegroom rejoiceth over the bride,
> So shall thy God rejoice over thee.   Isa. lxii.

The balance of the verses here is not only beautiful in itself, but by retarding the development of the thought, it allows each image to sink into the mind at leisure.   But naturally the same principle applies to parallelism as to the use of rhyme in poetry.   The thought must be worth putting into poetry, otherwise the verse calls attention to the poverty of idea.   For example, in Job xxxii, the tedious Elihu is made still more tedious by the parallelism, especially in the wearisome exordium:

> v. 11 Behold, I waited for your words,
>   I listened for your reasons,
>   Whilst ye searched out what to say.
>
>   12 Yea, I attended unto you,
>   And, behold, there was none that convinced Job,
>   Or that answered his words among you. . . .
>
>   16 And shall I wait, because they speak not,
>   Because they stand still, and answer no more.
>
>   17 I also will answer my part,
>   I also will show mine opinion . . .
>
>   20 I will speak, that I may be refreshed,
>   I will open my lips and answer.

This is prosy, but when the thought is sufficient great and elevated, the parallelism gives the composition its stateliness and solemnity:

> For he shall deliver thee from the snare of the fowler,
> And from the noisome pestilence.

> He shall cover thee with his pinions,
> And under his wings shalt thou take refuge.

> Thou shalt not be afraid for the terror by night,
> Nor for the arrow that flieth by day,

> For the pestilence that walketh in darkness,
> Nor for the destruction that wasteth at noonday.' Ps. xci. 3-6.

In the stately but mournful ninetieth Psalm, the effect of the parallelism resembles that of a half-muffled peal of bells, the second part of the verse supplying the tone of the answering peal:

> For we are consumed in thine anger,
> And in thy wrath are we troubled.

> Thou hast set our iniquities before thee,
> Our secret sins in the light of thy countenance.

> For all our days are passed away in thy wrath ;
> We bring our years to an end as a tale that is told.

> The days of our years are threescore years and ten,
> Or even by reason of strength fourscore years.

> Yet is their pride but labour and sorrow ;
> For it is soon gone, and we fly away . . . .

> Make us glad according to the days wherein thou hast afflicted us,
> And the years wherein we have seen evil.

> Let thy work appear unto thy servants,
> And thy glory upon their children.

> And let the beauty of the Lord our God be upon us,
> And establish thou the work of our hands upon us,
> Yea, the work of our hands establish thou it.

Further examples of parallelism may be found discussed in the account of Hebrew poetry given in Peake's *Commentary on the Bible* (T. & C. Jack).

Preparation (for lesson 15). Define the terms Humour and Irony. Write a short essay on national humour.

XII

Lesson 15

IRONY IN THE OLD TESTAMENT

'In these books we have not the laughter as well as the tears of humanity.'—Butcher, *Harvard Lectures*, p. 14.

WE should not expect the Old Testament, as the history and literature of the suffering nation,—a nation, too, of an oriental temperament,—to contain many instances of light humour and raillery. The humour that does appear is of that kind which adds to the distinction and vigour of a lofty style.

There is no laughter in it: it is an irony more or less grim. The laughter of the Old Testament is generally the laughter of scorn, like that of the incredulous Sarah,[1] or the derision the wicked will meet with in his fall.[2] Akin to this is the laughter of the exiles hearing of the decree for their return to Palestine, the hysterical laughter of people overjoyed and unable to credit the news.[3] The laughter of the Old Testament has the flavour of that 'sair' laughter with which a desperate and angry Scottish mob is said to have greeted the execution of one of their leaders. 'Even in laughter the heart is sorrowful, and the end of mirth is heaviness,' says the proverb.[4]

But irony is of the very essence of the Old Testament. There are characters, dialogues, and narratives which we remember chiefly for the sake of this irony.

The character of Samson, who has been called the wit of the Bible, is unthinkable without that sharp satire which reminds us of the intellectual strength so surprisingly

[1] Gen. xviii. 12, 13.
[2] Job xxii. 19, Ps. ii. 4, lix. 8.
[3] Ps. cxxvi. 2.
[4] Prov. xiv. 13.

combined with his physical prowess. A Hercules with a wit is a hero indeed. He not only slays his lion, but makes a good riddle about it, and he caps his victory over the Philistines with the snatch of a song.[1] He is credited with repartee, 'If ye had not ploughed with my heifer, ye had not found out my riddle'.[2] Considerable inventiveness is ascribed to him in the manner of his revenges, his practical jokes upon the Philistines.[3] The carrying off of the gates of Gaza in the presence of an ambush is something more than an exhibition of brute strength. In irony he mocks Delilah, and expresses the consciousness of his superiority, 'I will go out as at other times and *shake myself*'.[4]

The irony of Elijah at the expense of the prophets of Baal is the most memorable thing in the scene on Mount Carmel, 'Cry aloud, for he is a god; either he is musing, or he is gone aside, or he is on a journey, or peradventure he sleepeth, and must be awaked.' It has the effect of emphasizing the grimness of the struggle.[5]

In irony Isaiah denounces those who were mighty to 'drink wine', in drunken bouts,[6] and the strongest irony runs through the description of idolatry by the second Isaiah, 'A man heweth trees. He burneth part thereof in the fire; with part thereof he eateth flesh; he roasteth roast, and is satisfied; yea, he warmeth himself, and saith, "Aha, I am warm, I have seen the fire". And the residue thereof he maketh a god, even a graven image; he falleth down unto it, and worshippeth, and saith, " Deliver me, for thou art my god".'[7]

The irony of Job is well known. ' No doubt but ye are the people, and wisdom shall die with you.'[8] The Creator's reply to Job is full of it : 'Where is the way to the dwelling of light ? . . . Doubtless, thou knowest, for thou wast then born, and the number of thy days is great'.[9] 'Canst thou

---

[1] Judges xv. 16.   [2] Ibid., xiv. 18.   [3] Ibid., xv. 4, xvi. 3.
[4] Ibid., xvi. 20.   [5] I Kings xviii. 27.   [6] Isa. v. 22.
[7] Isa. xliv. 12-20, cf. also xlvii. 14.   [8] Job xii. 2.
[9] Job xxxviii. 19-21.

draw out Leviathan with a fish-hook, or press down his
tongue with a cord? . . . Wilt thou play with him as with
a bird? Or wilt thou bind him for thy maidens?'[1]

Such irony is the result of strong feeling, whether of
misery or of passionate indignation, so that even in the plays
on words or puns, and in the taunt-songs, which are so
peculiar a feature of the Old Testament, the irony does not
seem incongruous with a lofty style. The puns on names
which abound in the first chapter of Micah (e. g. 'In Gath
(= tell town) tell it not, in Akko (= weep town) weep not'),
and in certain chapters of Isaiah, are paralleled in English
and Greek tragedy. The best comment upon them is the
quotation which Farrar has made from Shakespeare, *King
Richard II*, 'Old Gaunt indeed, and gaunt in being old',
a pun which the dying man excuses by saying that 'misery
makes sport to mock itself'. The taunts are the only weapon
left to downtrodden Israel, with which to retaliate upon their
stronger but more brutish enemies. They are not mere bitter
curses; they are rather lofty judgements passed on other
peoples as from the mouth of God himself. Some of them
are magnificent, as, for instance, when the fall of Babylon
is the theme:

'Hell from beneath is moved for thee to meet thee at thy
coming: it stirreth up the dead for thee, even all the chief ones
of the earth: it hath raised up from their thrones all the kings
of the nations.

All they shall answer and say unto thee, 'Art thou also become
weak as we? Art thou become like unto us?'

Thy pomp is brought down to hell, and the noise of thy viols:
the worm is spread under thee, and worms cover thee.

How art thou fallen from heaven, O day star, son of the
morning! How art thou cut down to the ground, which didst
lay low the nations!

And thou saidst in thy heart, 'I will ascend into heaven, I will
exalt my throne above the stars of God . . .

Yet thou shalt be brought down to hell, to the uttermost parts
of the pit.

. They that see thee shall narrowly look upon thee, they shall
consider thee, saying, 'Is this the man that made the earth to
tremble, that did shake kingdoms, that made the world as

[1] Ibid., xli. 1, 5.

a wilderness, and overthrew the cities thereof; that let not loose
his prisoners to their home?'

All the kings of the nations, all of them, sleep in glory, every
one in his own house.

But thou art cast forth away from thy sepulchre like an
abominable branch ... as a carcase trodden under foot.

Thou shalt not be joined with them in burial, because thou
hast destroyed thy land, thou hast slain thy people; the seed of
evildoers shall not be named for ever.'   Isa. xiv. 9-20.

This picture of the kings in Hades rising up from their
thrones and peering (looking narrowly) at the newcomer,
their late oppressor, has always been admired for its dramatic
power. But it is the peculiar vein of irony with which we are
here concerned. Though the finger of scorn is pointed at
a fallen foe, the scorn is not mean, the exultation is strangely
chastened. The irony is in this case directed, not against
a personal or even a national enemy, but against the enemy
of the human race, whose senseless barbarity 'made the
world a wilderness', and did not respect the international
rights of prisoners. Babylon, which claimed to supersede
God in heaven, is after all mortal and food for worms.

So, too, in the ode of triumph, as in the Song of Deborah,
for instance, the irony is similarly restrained, and the personal
feeling promptly merged in the cause of Jehovah. 'So let all
thine enemies perish, O Lord, but let them that love him
be as the sun, when he goeth forth in his might.'

Exercise. Give instances of our Lord's use of irony from the Gospels.

Preparation (for lesson 16). Read Prov. iii. 11-20, the praise of wisdom,
and compare it with Job xxviii.

Read also Prov. xxxi. 10-end, 'the virtuous woman', (an acrostic
poem, each verse beginning with a letter of the Hebrew
alphabet).

Compare the scheme of Prov. xxx. 15-31 with the arrangement
of Amos's opening prophecy, Amos i. 3-ii. 6.

Or,

Learn by heart Prov. xxx. 24-28.

Lesson 16

The BOOKS of WISDOM

LITTLE has yet been quoted from the books of Wisdom, other than the books of Job and Ecclesiastes. A unique feature of the Old Testament is the collection of wise sayings styled Proverbs, and of the very brief essays, as they might be called, into which these were sometimes expanded, as in the book of Ecclesiastes, and the apocryphal books of Wisdom and Ecclesiasticus.

Proverbs and maxims are rather the germ of literature than literature itself. They are the texts or motives for longer compositions. They are usually ascribed to 'wise men', like the 'know thyself' of Solon the Athenian, but those who are familiar with such mother wit as that of Mrs. Poyser in *Adam Bede*, and the type of epigram it produces, will see how shrewd reflections can be issued in the rough, before they pass through the mint of more polished wits, get beaten into small coin, and go out stamped as suitable currency. Among the Hebrews there was actually a class of such wits or wise men, who played the author to such wisdom as was to be found in a reflective people. These wise men ranked with the prophets and priests (see Jer. xviii. 18, Prov. xxii. 17), though their tone was more secular, and their views often less orthodox.

Here we are concerned less with their views than with the literary features of their writings. The features already discussed are even more strongly pronounced in these writings, if possible, viz. the use of simile, metaphor,

personification, &c.   It is the aptness or striking nature of
the simile or analogy that in many cases makes the proverb :

> As a jewel of gold in a swine's snout,
> So is a fair woman which is without discretion.   Prov. xi. 22.

> The hoary head is a crown of glory,
> If it be found in the way of righteousness.   Prov. xvi. 31.

> As cold waters to a thirsty soul,
> So is good news from a far country.   Prov. xxv. 25.

> A continual dropping in a very rainy day
> And a contentious woman are alike.   Prov. xxvii. 15.

So it is with metaphor :

> If thine enemy be hungry, give him bread to eat, . . .
> For thou shalt *heap coals of fire upon his head*.   Prov. xxv. 21, 22.

and with hyperbole :

> Though thou shouldest bray a fool in a mortar with a pestle
>   among bruised corn,
> Yet will not his foolishness depart from him.   Prov. xxvii. 22.

The *diction* of a maxim will naturally be concise in the
extreme, and language could scarcely be reduced to lower
terms than in

> The heaven for height, and the earth for depth,
> And the heart of kings is unsearchable.   Prov. xxv. 3.

> As in water face (answereth) to face,
> So the heart of man to man.   Prov. xxvii. 19.

Personification is carried so far in the representation of
Wisdom, that by some the writer has been thought to have
conceived her as a personal being distinct from God himself.

> The Lord possessed me in the beginning of his way,
> Before his works of old.

> When there were no depths, I was brought forth ;
> .   .   .   .
> When he established the heavens, I was there,
> .   .   .   .
> Then I was by him, as a master workman :
> And I was daily his delight,
> Rejoicing always before him.   Prov. viii. 22 ff.

Again, in virtue of their *parallelism,* these writings rank as poetry.   Some of the Psalms, in fact, are themselves classed among the poems of Wisdom, and differ little in matter and style.   Psalm i, for instance, has much in common with Proverbs xxviii. 5, 6, 7, 25, 28, but it has internal unity, while the Proverbs are detached verses.

Proverbs are, of course, frequently grouped together to illustrate one thought, as in the picturesque description of the sluggard :

> The sluggard saith, There is a lion in the way,
> A lion is in the streets.
>
> As the door turneth upon its hinges,
> So doth the sluggard upon his bed.
>
> The sluggard burieth his hand in the dish ;
> It wearieth him to bring it again to his mouth.
>
> The sluggard is wiser in his own conceit
> Than seven men that can render a reason.   Prov. xxvi. 13-16.

Often they show some progression from verse to verse, and treat of a particular theme, e. g. wine :

> Look not thou upon the wine when it is red, . . .
> At the last it biteth like a serpent, . . .
> Thine eyes shall behold strange things, . . .
> Yea, thou shalt be as he that lieth down in the midst of the sea, . . .
> They have stricken me, (thou shalt say), and I was not hurt ; . . .
> When shall I awake ?   I will seek it yet again.
>   Prov. xxiii. 31–35.

A still further stage is reached with Ecclesiastes, and Ecclesiasticus, which, though much broken and disjointed, contain the rudiments of the essay.   Of these we will print in full two examples from Wisdom and Ecclesiasticus respectively, as they are in the Apocrypha, and less accessible.

Wisdom v.

(A very fine passage, with some remarkable similes, and in vv. 18, 19 imagery used afterwards by St. Paul, Eph. vi. 14–17, and previously by Isaiah lix. 17.   The author of this book is a great believer in the rewards appointed for the righteous in a future life, and expounds the doctrine of immortality.)

1 Then shall the righteous man stand in great boldness before the face of such as have afflicted him, and made no account of his labours.

2 When they see it, they shall be troubled with terrible fear, and shall be amazed at the strangeness of his salvation, so far beyond all that they looked for.

3 And they repenting and groaning for anguish of spirit shall say within themselves, This was he whom we had sometimes in derision, and a proverb of reproach :

4 We fools accounted his life madness, and his end to be without honour :

5 How is he numbered among the children of God, and his lot is among the saints !

6 Therefore have we erred from the way of truth, and the light of righteousness hath not shined unto us, and the sun of righteousness rose not upon us.

7 We wearied ourselves in the way of wickedness and destruction : yea, we have gone through deserts, where there lay no way : but as for the way of the Lord, we have not known it.

8 What hath pride profited us ? or what good hath riches with our vaunting brought us ?

9 All those things are passed away like a shadow, and as a post that hasted by ;

10 And as a ship that passeth over the waves of the water, which when it is gone by, the trace thereof cannot be found, neither the pathway of the keel in the waves ;

11 Or as when a bird hath flown through the air, there is no token of her way to be found, but the light air being beaten with the stroke of her wings, and parted with the violent noise and motion of them, is passed through, and therein afterwards no sign where she went is to be found ;

12 Or like as when an arrow is shot at a mark, it parteth the air, which immediately cometh together again, so that a man cannot know where it went through :

13 Even so we in like manner, as soon as we were born, began to draw to our end, and had no sign of virtue to show ; but were consumed in our own wickedness.

14 For the hope of the ungodly is like dust that is blown away with the wind ; like a thin froth that is driven away with the storm, like as the smoke that is dispersed here and there with a tempest, and passeth away as the remembrance of a guest that tarrieth but a day.

15 But the righteous live for evermore ; their reward also is with the Lord, and the care of them is with the most High.

16 Therefore shall they receive a glorious kingdom, and a beautiful crown from the Lord's hand ; for with his right hand shall he cover them, and with his arm shall he protect them.

Then come the verses which, in an extended form, St. Paul applies to the Christian in Ephesians.

18 He shall put on righteousness as a breastplate, and true judgment instead of an helmet.
19 He shall take holiness for an invincible shield.
20 His severe wrath shall he sharpen for a sword, and the world shall fight with him against the unwise.

The other passage from Ecclesiasticus (xliv) is commonly read at Commemoration Services and on Foundation Days.

1 Let us now praise famous men, and our fathers that begat us.
2 The Lord hath wrought great glory by them through his great power from the beginning.
3 Such as did bear rule in their kingdoms, men renowned for their power, giving counsel by their understanding, and declaring prophecies:
4 Leaders of the people by their counsels, and by their knowledge of learning meet for the people, wise and eloquent in their instructions:
5 Such as found out musical tunes, and recited verses in writing:
6 Rich men furnished with ability, living peaceably in their habitations:
7 All these were honoured in their generations, and were the glory of their times.
8 There be of them that have left a name behind them, that their praises might be reported.
9 And some there be, which have no memorial; who are perished as though they had never been; and are become as though they had never been born; and their children after them.
10 But these were merciful men, whose righteousness hath not been forgotten.
11 With their seed shall continually remain a good inheritance, and their children are within the covenant.
12 Their seed standeth fast, and their children for their sakes.
13 Their seed shall remain for ever, and their glory shall not be blotted out.
14 Their bodies are buried in peace; but their name liveth for evermore.
15 The people will tell of their wisdom, and the congregation will shew forth their praise.

Lesson *17*

The *STYLE of the OLD TESTAMENT continued in the NEW*

IF it is remembered that the Old Testament began to assume its permanent form after the Exile, and that books were still being added to it in the first century B. C., it is not surprising that Jesus Christ, himself a Jew, brought up in the synagogue, in speaking to Jewish audiences should have to some extent continued the tradition of Hebrew literature, and however unique and fresh his teaching, have reproduced in his style and methods many features of the Old Testament writings. Nor is it strange that Mark, the originator of a new type of literature, the Gospel, thinking and writing as a Jew and under the influence of Peter, should have cast his narrative in a form for which all Jewish readers would be prepared, that of memoirs.

I. Take the second point first, the form of St. Mark's Gospel, based, it must be remembered, on oral teaching, so that all but the most memorable sayings and doings of Jesus would be forgotten. In writing memoirs Mark was following the biographical method of the Old Testament, which gives us, for instance, the sayings and doings of Elijah and Elisha, and incidents from the life of Samuel and Saul, not full and complete biographies, recording events as they happened year by year, with dates and documents. So Mark gives us a memoir, not a biography. A biography after the modern manner in two or three volumes would have had less chance of surviving, certainly a far less wide circulation. Memoirs preserve the personality of their subject through his most striking sayings and doings. It is personality that people wish to hear about, and the handy, lively Gospel of Mark goes all over the world to-day, and is within reach of the poorest.

But more than this, Mark followed the brief, simple, direct style of the Old Testament, records incidents without comment, avoids elaboration and artificiality of every kind, and suppresses emotion. The similarity of style will appear from the following examples:

Death of Saul.

1 Sam. xxxi. 3-6, 8-13.

And the battle went sore against Saul, and the archers overtook him; and he was greatly distressed by reason of the archers.

Then said Saul to his armourbearer, Draw thy sword, and thrust me through therewith; lest these uncircumcised come and thrust me through, and abuse me.

But his armourbearer would not; for he was sore afraid. Therefore Saul took his sword, and fell upon it.

And when his armourbearer saw that Saul was dead, he likewise fell upon his sword, and died with him. . . .

And it came to pass on the morrow, when the Philistines came to strip the slain, that they found Saul and his three sons fallen in Mount Gilboa.

And they cut off his head, and stripped off his armour, and sent into the land of the Philistines round about, to carry the tidings unto the house of their idols, and to the people.

And they put his armour in the house of the Astaroth: and they fastened his body to the wall of Beth-shan.

Death of John the Baptist.

Mark vi. 21-29.

And when a convenient day was come, that Herod on his birthday made a supper to his lords, and the high captains, and the chief men of Galilee;

And when the daughter of Herodias herself came in and danced, she pleased Herod and them that sat at meat with him; and the king said unto the damsel, Ask of me whatsoever thou wilt, and I will give it thee.

And he sware unto her, Whatsoever thou shalt ask of me, I will give it thee, unto the half of my kingdom.

And she went out and said unto her mother, What shall I ask? And she said, The head of John the Baptist.

And she came in straightway with haste unto the king, and asked, saying, I will that thou forthwith give me in a charger the head of John the Baptist.

And the king was exceeding sorry; but for the sake of his oaths, and of them that sat at meat, he would not reject her.

And straightway the king sent forth a soldier of the guard, and commanded to bring his head: and he went and beheaded him in the prison,

And when the inhabitants of Jabesh-gilead heard concerning him that which the Philistines had done to Saul,

All the valiant men arose, and went all night, and took the body of Saul and the bodies of his sons from the wall of Beth-shan; and they came to Jabesh, and burnt them there.

And they took their bones, and buried them under the tamarisk tree in Jabesh, and fasted seven days.

And brought his head in a charger, and gave it to the damsel; and the damsel gave it to her mother.

And when the disciples heard thereof, they came and took up his corpse, and laid it in a tomb.

The plain, straightforward narrative, the effect of the dialogue, and the absence of comment upon the treatment of the two great men, are features of both accounts. The last verses in each case are specially to be noticed. The deed is told, emotions are suppressed. The cruelty of the doers, the grief of the disciples at the loss of their great master, the devotion of the men of Jabesh-gilead, are all left to be inferred with a reticence that is wonderfully effective.

The same is true of the account of Christ's miracles. The style is very like that of Kings, where Elisha's miracles are told. Compare the brevity and vigour of each of the following accounts, especially of the last verse:

The Poisonous Pot.
2 Kings iv. 38–41.

38 And Elisha came again to Gilgal: and there was a dearth in the land; and the sons of the prophets were sitting before him: and he said unto his servant, Set on the great pot, and seethe pottage for the sons of the prophets.

39 And one went out into the field to gather herbs, and found a wild vine, and gathered thereof wild gourds his lap full, and came and shred them into the pot of pottage: for they knew them not.

40 So they poured out for the

The Man with the Withered Hand.
St. Mark iii. 1–5.

1 And he entered again into the synagogue; and there was a man there which had his hand withered.

2 And they watched him, whether he would heal him on the sabbath day; that they might accuse him.

3 And he saith unto the man that had his hand withered, Stand forth.

4 And he saith unto them, Is it lawful on the sabbath day to do good, or to do harm? to save a life, or to kill? But they held their peace.

men to eat. And it came to pass, as they were eating of the pottage, that they cried out and said, O man of God, there is death in the pot. And they could not eat thereof.

41 But he said, Then bring meal. And he cast it into the pot; and he said, Pour out for the people, that they may eat. And there was no harm in the pot.

5 And when he had looked round about on them with anger, being grieved at the hardening of their heart, he saith unto the man, Stretch forth thy hand. And he stretched it forth: and his hand was restored.

Compare especially v. 41 of the first account with the second part of v. 5 in the second. 2 Kings iv. 41-44 may also be compared with Mark vi. 35-43, only of course in respect of style, though there are incidental correspondences of matter too.

What applies to Mark, also applies to Matthew and Luke. Luke follows the Old Testament in another respect, viz. in his introduction of Psalms into his narrative, the Magnificat corresponding very closely to the Song of Hannah in 1 Sam. ii.

II. Secondly, examine the teaching of Jesus. Unique as it is, it uses the armoury of the prophets, simile, metaphor, parable, allegory, wise sayings in proverb and epigram, denunciation and appeal, and even lamentation. There is often the same note of irony moreover.

Similes are used occasionally:

'As the lightning cometh forth from the east, and is seen even unto the west, so shall be the coming of the Son of man.'
Matt. xxiv. 27.

and there are striking *metaphors*:

'Neither cast ye your pearls before swine . . .'
'Cast out the beam out of thine own eye . . .'
'He that gathereth not with me, scattereth . . .', &c., &c.

but it is in the *analogies* and *parables* that one sees the resemblance to the manner of the Old Testament most clearly:

Isa. i. 3.

'The ox knoweth his owner, and the ass his master's crib, but Israel doth not know, my people doth not consider.'

Luke ix. 58.

'The foxes have holes, and the birds of the heaven have nests, but the Son of man hath not where to lay his head.'

The Vineyard.

Isa. v. 1-5.

1 My wellbeloved had a vineyard in a very fruitful hill :

2 And he made a trench about it, and gathered out the stones thereof, and planted it with the choicest vine, and built a tower in the midst of it, and also hewed out a winepress therein, and he looked that it should bring forth grapes, and it brought forth wild grapes.

. . . .

3 And now ... judge, I pray you, betwixt me and my vineyard.

4 What could have been done more to my vineyard, that I have not done in it ?

5 And now go to, I will tell you what I will do to my vineyard : I will take away the hedge thereof, and it shall be eaten up ...

The Wicked Husbandmen.

Matt. xxi. 33-41.

33 There was a man that was a householder, which planted a vineyard, and set a hedge about it, and digged a winepress in it, and built a tower, and let it out to husbandmen, and went into another country.

34 And when the season of the fruits drew near, he sent his servants to the husbandmen, to receive his fruits.

. . . .

40 When therefore the lord of the vineyard shall come, what will he do unto those husbandmen ?
(Note the question addressed to the audience in each case.)

41 He will miserably destroy those miserable men, and will let out the vineyard unto other husbandmen ...

Rhetorical questions are too frequent to need quoting, but those that contain similes remind us of the questions propounded by Amos and Isaiah :

'Shall two walk together, except they have agreed?' Amos iii. 3.

'Can a woman forget her child ...?' Isa. xlix. 15.

'Can the blind guide the blind? shall they not both fall into a pit?' Luke vi. 39.

'Are not two sparrows sold for a farthing? Ye are of more value ...' Matt. x. 29.

'Is the lamp brought to be put under the bushel ...?'

Mark iv. 21.

Hyperboles :

'The very hairs of your head are all numbered.' Matt. x. 30.

'It is easier for a camel to enter in through a needle's eye, than for a rich man to enter into the kingdom of God.'

Luke xviii. 25.

'If any man cometh unto me, and hateth not his own father, and mother, . . . he cannot be my disciple.'   Luke xiv. 26.

'If ye have faith as a grain of mustard seed, ye would say unto this sycamine tree, Be thou rooted up, and be thou planted in the sea; and it would have obeyed you.'   Luke xvii. 6.

The *aphorisms* of Jesus recall the Wisdom literature of the Old Testament, especially Proverbs and Ecclesiastes:

'He that hath, to him shall be given . . .'   Mark iv. 25.

'He that findeth his life shall lose it,
And he that loseth his life for my sake shall find it.'   Matt. x. 39.

'Everyone that exalteth himself shall be humbled,
And he that humbleth himself, shall be exalted.'   Luke xiv. 11.

'There are last which shall be first,
and there are first which shall be last.'   Luke xiii. 30.

These have been called 'seed-thoughts'. Notice the balance of the two parts of the verse, as in Proverbs. When the verse is expanded into a paragraph, its form and arrangement recall the little paragraphs of wisdom in Ecclesiastes.

Eccles. v. 4, 5.	Matt. vi. 5, 6.
'When thou vowest a vow unto God, defer not to pay it; for he hath no pleasure in fools: pay that which thou vowest. . . .	'When ye pray, ye shall not be as the hypocrites: for they love to stand and pray in the synagogues and in the corners of the streets. . . .

The prophet's *appeal* to his audience strikes the same note:

'Come unto me, all ye that labour, and are heavy laden, and I will give you rest. Take my yoke upon you, and learn of me; . . . and ye shall find rest unto your souls.'   Matt. xi. 28.

with which we may compare Isaiah lv. 1–3.

'Ho, every one that thirsteth, come ye to the waters. . . . Incline your ear, and come unto me; hear, and your soul shall live.'

When under the stress of emotion, Jesus falls naturally into the expression and balanced style of the prophets:

'O Jerusalem, Jerusalem, which killeth the prophets,
and stoneth them that are sent unto her!
how often would I have gathered thy children together,
even as a hen gathereth her own brood under her wings,
and ye would not!
Behold, your house is left unto you desolate:
and I say unto you,
Ye shall not see me, until ye shall say,
Blessed is he that cometh in the name of the Lord.'
Luke xiii. 34, 35.

'If thou hadst known in this day, even thou,
the things which belong unto peace!
but now they are hid from thine eyes.

For the days shall come upon thee,
when thine enemies shall cast up a bank about thee,
and compass thee round,
and keep thee in on every side,

and shall dash thee to the ground,
and thy children within thee;

and they shall not leave in thee one stone upon another,
because thou knewest not the time of thy visitation.'

Luke xix. 42-4.

'Daughters of Jerusalem, weep not for me,
but weep for yourselves, and for your children.

For behold, the days are coming,
in which they shall say,

Blessed are the barren, and the wombs that never bare,
and the breasts that never gave suck.

Then shall they begin to say to the mountains, Fall on us,
and to the hills, Cover us.

For if they do these things in the green tree,
what shall be done in the dry?'   Luke xxiii. 28-31.

The *denunciations* of the Scribes and Pharisees recall the prophets' denunciations of the wickedness of the surrounding peoples and of their own.   Compare Isaiah v. 8-24 with Matt. xxiii. 13-36, and Jer. xlvi-li with Matt. xi. 20-24.

Nor are instances of the *irony* of the Old Testament wanting in the speech of Christ, whether of the sterner type, as when he reproaches the Pharisees who 'strain at the gnat, and swallow the camel', or tells the man who offers to follow him to 'let the dead bury their dead', or asks the Pharisees before the man with the withered hand whether it is lawful to save life on the Sabbath day or to kill—or again of the gentler kind, as when he playfully tells the Syrophoenician woman that 'it is not meet to take the children's bread and cast it to the dogs', and receives the witty retort that pleases him so. Lastly, in the manner of the Old Testament, he puns upon

Peter's name, 'Thou art Peter, and upon this rock (Greek, *petra*) I will build my church.'

Note.—When we pass from the synoptic gospels, we 'emerge into a fresh world.' The fourth gospel bears the mark of Greek influences, and contains discourses of a new type, long and argumentative. But it is the epistles of St. Paul, with their brilliant reasoning and literary art, which 'announce unmistakably that we have now left behind us the mental habits and limitations of the Old Testament writers. (Prof. Hudson, Peake's *Commentary*, who also quotes Gardiner, *The Bible as English Literature*, 'When we pass from Proverbs and Job to St. John and Romans and Hebrews, we have passed from the world of Solomon to the world of Socrates.')

Lesson 18

SELECTED PASSAGES for ADDITIONAL STUDY

THE following passages may also be examined for their literary beauty. Some reasons for admiring them are suggested in each case.

Ecclesiastes xii. 1–7.

The preacher describing the coming decay of old age, shows it through the soft haze of a series of images or symbols, some of which are not very intelligible to us, while others we have borrowed for our own use.

The passage is a good example of the way in which the metaphors pour out from the rich Oriental imagination. The effect of them is to make tender and beautiful a melancholy, which in the rest of the book tends to be bitter and hard.

1 Remember also thy Creator in the days of thy youth, or ever the evil days come, and the years draw nigh, when thou shalt say, I have no pleasure in them ;

2 or ever the sun, and the light, and the moon, and the stars, be darkened, and the clouds return after the rain : [1]

3 in the day when the keepers of the house [2] shall tremble, and the strong men [3] shall bow themselves, and the grinders [4] cease because they are few, and those that look out of the windows be darkened, [5]

4 and the doors [6] shall be shut in the street ; when the sound of the grinding is low, [7] and one shall rise up at the voice of the bird, [8] and all the daughters of music shall be brought low : [9]

Notes.

[1] Life begins to lose its brightness, and the showers are not followed by sunshine but only more clouds.

[2] In v. 3 the body is compared with a house and its inmates, menfolk, women who grind as servants, and ladies who look out of the windows. The arms [2] and legs [3] grow weak, and the teeth [4] (lit. grinding women) and the eyes [5] (those that look out of the window) fail ; the lips [6] are closed, mastication [7] is feeble.

5 Yea, they shall be afraid of that which is high,[10] and terrors shall be in the way;[11] and the almond tree shall flourish,[12] and the grasshopper shall be a burden,[13] and desire shall fail,[14] because man goeth to his long home, and the mourners go about the streets:

† [8] The old man wakes up with the early twitter of birds, and singers[9] are all alike low to him in his deafness.
[10] He is afraid of hills, and [11]journeys, being short of breath.
[12] (Meaning uncertain.)
[13] The smallest thing is a burden (cf. Isa. xl. 22.)
[14] Appetite fails.

6 or ever the silver cord be loosed, or the golden bowl be broken, or the pitcher be broken at the fountain, or the wheel broken at the cistern;
7 and the dust return to the earth as it was, and the spirit return unto God who gave it.

The time comes when the thread of life snaps like the silver cord, that holds up the golden lamp bowl, and the lamp falls and the light goes out; so, in homelier metaphor, the water of life is spilt, when the pitcher breaks.

Job xxviii.

The writer here sets out to describe the highest wisdom. His method is worth studying. He tells us first what wisdom is not; and where the way of perfect wisdom does not lie. The *miner* for all his wonderful skill, burrowing in the bowels of the earth and bringing up all sorts of treasures, does not come near wisdom. The *sea* is not deep enough to contain it. No *precious stone* can buy it or compare with it. The most *keen-eyed birds*, no living thing in fact, has descried it. It belongs to God alone, who balances all the forces of nature. 'When he made a decree for the rain, and a way for the lightning of the thunder', then it was God contemplated wisdom and expressed it, the reflection of himself, as it were, in his own creation. From that time wisdom for men could only mean one thing, the fear of God, who had expressed perfect wisdom.

† The meaning is uncertain. Another suggestion is 'He shall approach to the voice of a bird', i. e. his voice becomes shrill and piping.

These notes are taken in the main from the explanations of Principal A. J. Grieve, Peake's *Commentary on the Bible*, p. 417.

H

The passage is too long to print in full, but the revised version of vv. 1–4 is here given, and should be compared with the authorized version, which is unintelligible.

1   Surely there is a mine for silver,
     And a place for gold which they refine.
2   Iron is taken out of the earth,
     And brass is molten out of the stone.
3   *Man* setteth an end to darkness,
     And searcheth out to the furthest bound
     The stones of thick darkness and of the
     shadow of death.

> i. e. the miner, with his lamp, and so can search the depths.

4   He breaketh open a shaft away from
     where men sojourn ;
     They are forgotten of the foot *that*
     passeth by ;
     They hang afar from men, they swing
     to and fro.

> i. e. (if the reading is properly amended), he opens a shaft . . . and hangs swinging on a rope.

.   .   .   .

7   (Read) *That* path no bird . . . . knoweth.
(This and the next verse some scholars would like to put after 12, and it would then mean the path of wisdom, not the path of the miner.)

> In v. 5 the meaning is that the corn grows quietly above, while blasting goes on below.
>
> vv. 9–11 complete the description of mining.

Notice

1. The refrain dividing the chapter into three parts. It has been suggested that the poem also began with it, as the opening words in the Hebrew imply that another previous sentence has dropped out. 'Where shall wisdom be found ? . . . For there is a mine for silver ', &c.

2. The simple and majestic diction. The recital of metals and jewels, as they are compared and rejected in turn, postpones the climax and adds force to the revelation when it comes in the final 'strophe'.

3. The difficulty of fitting in the poem with the argument of the chapters before and after has led scholars to regard it as an independent poem, which has found its way in somehow to the text of Job. Compare Proverbs viii. The last verse is similarly regarded as the addition of some scribe, on the ground that it speaks of wisdom as possible for man to attain, contrary to the tenour of

the rest of the chapter, which treats of wisdom as belonging only to God. See a similar addition in Eccles. xii. 13. (Franks, Peake's *Commentary*, p. 359.)

Isaiah i. 1–26.

is an excellent example of oratory, and has been called the Great Arraignment. The variety of address will be noticed, command, exclamation, question, pleading, and fierce invective rapidly succeeding one another. The following phrases may be selected for their imagery or the terse expressiveness of their diction :

v. 3 The ox knoweth his owner, and the ass his master's crib :
　　But Israel doth not know, my people doth not consider.'

　5 The whole head is sick, and the whole heart faint.

18 Come now, and let us reason together, saith the Lord :
　　Though your sins be as scarlet, they shall be as white
　　　as snow,
　　Though they be red like crimson, they shall be as wool.

22 Thy silver is become dross.

24 Ah, I will ease me of mine adversaries.

Psalm xxiii.

is another instance (like Psalm lxxx) of the use of metaphor extended after the manner of an allegory, here drawn from the picturesqueness of shepherd life. Its beauty has always been admired.

APPENDIX

NOTES on EXERCISES

i. *Elisha's story less dramatic than that of Elijah*, p. 40.

(*a*) Elijah lives aloof; Elisha is often in the towns, and near the court, in touch with the king, to whom he acts as adviser, and with whom he is on good terms, whereas Elijah was in conflict with the court. Gentle correction and continuous advice replace grand remonstrance and denunciation.

(*b*) Elisha's antecedents are mentioned, his family, and his call from his estate; no mention is made of Elijah's circumstances. He is like Melchisedek, has 'no beginning of days' (Heb. vii. 3), and is too saintly to die. Elisha's death-bed scene is described.

(*c*) The most dramatic thing in the ministry of Elisha is initiated by him through a messenger, viz. the revolt of Jehu.

ii. *The vision of Ezekiel compared with that of Isaiah and that of Moses*, p. 49.

Notice the elaborate and complicated nature of Ezekiel's vision, and compare the simple and majestic way in which the two first visions make one feel the mystery of the divine presence.

The symbolism of Ezekiel is weird, if not grotesque: compare the wings and wheels belonging to the same creatures, and *eyes* in the wheels. The creatures themselves, with their four wings and four faces, were probably suggested by the curious figures of Babylonian art. Ezekiel alone tries to be at all explicit in describing God himself, and gives him 'a likeness as the appearance of a man'. See especially vv. 6–11, 18, 26. The elaborate description of the chariot and the wheels is to represent the omniscience, omnipresence, and omnipotence of God. The more sublime accounts of visions have little use for this detailed symbolism.

iii. *Amos* iii. 3–8, p. 49. A number of analogies from nature illustrating the law of cause and effect. Every phenomenon has its cause ; if two men are seen walking together in the desert, it is because they have made an arrangement to do so. If a lion roars, it is because he scents some prey ; if a young lion growls from his den, it is because he has captured his prey. . . . If a trumpet is blown in a city, it is because of some alarm. And so also when evil befalls a city, it is due to God's action ; and if a prophet is moved to prophesy, it is due to God's summons, and because he has told them his secret.

iv. *The allegory in Ezekiel* xix. 10–14, p. 58.
Here, too, Israel is compared with a vine, but the comparison is less striking and poetical.

(1) Compare particularly vv. 10, 11, describing the growth of the vine, with the fine expressions in vv. 9–11 of the Psalm.

(2) Notice the repetition of 'branches' and 'rods', vv. 10, 11, 12, 14. Ezekiel is given to repetition.

(3) The east wind drying up the vine is a less effective image than the wild boar in the Psalm, representing the brute force of Assyria trampling the small nation underfoot.

v. *Job* xxvi. 6–14, p. 61. *A survey of the universe, to show the infinity of God.* It begins with Hades, which is open to God ; and the next marvel is the North or place of the great mountains, as it was thought by the Jews, hanging in chaos and resting on nothing, in spite of its weight.

In v. 8, the image is that of water bound up in skins, without bursting the skins, the 'bottles of heaven' or the clouds, as in xxxviii. 37.

v. 10 gives us the Babylonian idea of the earth as a flat disc resting on chaos, an ocean of waters, with the vault of heaven rising over it, the firmament of light, while all outside is darkness.

v. 11. The pillars of heaven are the mountains, rising from

the edge of the disc, to support the vault of heaven, while their roots go down into chaos.

v. 12. Rahab is the chaos monster, and in v. 13 the swift serpent is Leviathan (cf. iii. 8).

v. 13. This refers to the clearing of the storm-clouds, so that the heavens are bright (garnished) by his breath (spirit). (Franks, Peake's *Commentary*, p. 359.)

In spite of the ancient conception of the universe, the imagery commands admiration as usual, closing with the fine phrases of v. 14:

> These are but the outskirts of his ways;
> And *how small a whisper do we hear of him !*

vi. *Isaiah xlix and Zechariah viii compared*, p. 72.

Both dwell on the re-peopling of Jerusalem. Zechariah confines himself to possible consequences, and gives a homely picture, vv. 4, 5, 7, 8. The vine shall give her fruit, and the people, though a remnant, will inherit this good fortune.

Isaiah substitutes for the plain people of Zechariah the 'children of her bereavement', whom the city will 'wear as a bride wears ornaments', vv. 18–20. Kings and queens should come and bow down to Zion, and nurse her children, vv. 22, 23. Then instead of the plain prosperity of the land, Isaiah gives an ideal picture of the restored country:

'On all bare heights shall be their pasture . . . even by the springs of water shall he guide them', vv. 9–11. Nature is then called upon to rejoice and sing in company.

In their appeals to their audiences for faith, Zechariah again uses plain language, v. 6, Isaiah uses a simile, v. 15, both put in the form of a question. So, too, in describing the fame of the future Jerusalem, Zechariah (vv. 21–3) says with extraordinary plainness and realism, 'ten men shall *take hold of the skirt of him* that is a Jew, saying, We will go with you, for we have heard that God is with you.' Isaiah again uses imagery, 'Behold, I will lift up mine hand to the nations, and *set up my ensign* to the peoples: and they shall *bring thy sons in their bosom*, and thy daughters shall be *carried upon their shoulders*', v. 22; '*Kings* shall see and arise; *princes*, and they shall worship; because of the Lord that is faithful. . . .'

vii. *Isaiah lix. Progression of imagery*, p. 72.

v. 4 They *conceive* mischief and *bring forth* iniquity.

A general metaphorical expression.

This in v. 5 becomes the special metaphor:

> They *hatch* basilisks' *eggs*, (and weave the spider's *web*.)

The second of these images is, in its turn, developed in the next sentence:

> Their *webs* shall not become *garments*,
> Neither shall they *cover themselves* with their works.

Garments suggested 'covering', and the final word 'works' suggests the next thought:

> Their works are works of iniquity,
> and the act of violence is in their *hands*.

Here 'works' suggests its synonym 'act', and 'hands' suggest 'feet' in the next sentence:

> Their *feet* run to evil. . . .
> Desolation and destruction are in their *paths*.

where again 'paths' suggest '*way* of peace' which follows.

v. 9. The general metaphor 'walk in obscurity' suggests the special one in the next verse 'grope for the wall', followed by 'stumble at noon-day'.

v. 16. 'Righteousness' is followed by the simile 'put on righteousness as a breastplate', and again by 'put on garments of vengeance', while the word 'vengeance' again suggests 'repay' in the following verse.

The reader is gently borne on by the sequence of ideas, and the passage is built up step by step unawares.

viii. *Judges v. Reconstruction of the battle*, p. 77.

R. G. Moulton gives the following account of the battle in his *Literary Study of the Bible*:

The oppression of Jabin had been so violent that the main roads were not safe for the Jews to use, v. 6. The people had been disarmed, and had to fight with what they could get. Their only hope lay in a surprise, for Jabin had nine hundred chariots of iron. They arranged for a quiet muster on high ground by Kedesh, and watched for a favourable moment to make a rapid descent on the enemy. (Heber the Kenite betrayed the plan, ch. iv. 11, 12.) Sisera poured his full forces on to the plain of Esdraelon, where his chariots could move freely. But 'the stars in their courses fought against Sisera'. A storm came on, the river Kishon overflowed, and swept down in a torrent, and flooded the plain, and helped on the discomfiture of the host, and the horses floundered about in the water and mud, vv. 20–22, and presumably the charge of the half-armed highlanders did its work.

The singer also comments on the conduct of those tribes who did not join the revolt. Meroz, for instance, a city on the line of the enemy's retreat, is cursed for not coming to help, v. 23. Reuben could not make up its mind to the risk, v. 16. The cowards and the brave are contrasted in vv. 17 and 18.

The muster is described in vv. 14–19, the battle in vv. 20–23, and the punishment of Sisera and the anxiety of his Court in the last part of the song.

INDEX